The Bible for Every Day

ABRAHAM

The Revd Ronald S. Wallace studied at Edinburgh University, gaining his Ph.D. in 1958. He was a minister of several Church of Scotland parishes before becoming Professor of Biblical Theology at Columbia Theological Seminary in the United States, a position he held for thirteen years until his retirement. He now lives in Edinburgh, where he devotes his time to writing. *The Bible for Every Day*, the distillation of a lifetime's experience of teaching the Bible to Church congregations and to theological students, reflects his unique blend of scholarship and spiritual insight.

D1646116

The Bible for Every Day
by Ronald S. Wallace

ABRAHAM   GENESIS 12—23

In Preparation
ISAAC AND JACOB   GENESIS 24—36
JOSEPH   GENESIS 37—50

ABRAHAM

Genesis 12—23

Ronald S. Wallace

TRIANGLE

SPCK

First published 1981
Triangle
SPCK
Holy Trinity Church
Marylebone Road
London NW1 4DU

Filmset, printed and bound in Great Britain by
Hazell Watson & Viney Ltd, Aylesbury, Bucks

ISBN 0 281 03808 2

To
Grace and Claude Gibson
and the people of Ramsay Memorial
Alabama

Contents

CONTENTS

CONTENTS

Introduction

Throughout my earlier parish ministry I had many interested lay people, some receptive, some critical (I do not know to which I am most indebted) who came to church services to hear the Word of God interpreted in its relevance especially to our personal lives, but also to the Church and the world. They believed, as I did, that Christ himself comes into the midst today to enable us to understand the Scriptures within the fellowship of his people, as he did on the road to Emmaus, and they expected to hear his voice. They were willing to gather in small groups to discuss passages with me and with one another.

When I later became a theological teacher, I was able to devote much more time to the study of the current and traditional exegetical and critical discussion amongst scholars, and I became better informed on background and historical matters. But when I tried to convey all this to my students in an academic way, I was unhappy. Some of them knew the languages better than I could remember, and in any case, with little trouble most of them could find everything I was trying to convey to them in other people's commentaries.

I decided, therefore, to return to what I had previously been used to doing, and knew better—and to try to do it more expertly now, and as much as possible to the standard of scholarship expected within an academic environment.

For the warm response of the students I shall always be grateful. They came now in comparatively large numbers, with their wives, and other lay people and pastors—and with the same kind of desire to hear and willingness to listen as I had previously found in a congregation.

The books in this series are the product of this continuing ministry. But instead of taking the form of textual sermons or a series of lectures, they have been arranged to take the

reader continuously through the printed biblical text, sometimes from chapter to chapter, sometimes from oracle to
oracle, sometimes from incident to incident and sometimes
from verse to verse, following the order of the text, and
trying not to leave out what is important or what might be
difficult. They are arranged in easily readable units divided
by carefully chosen headings. This arrangement will enable
those who customarily have a daily Bible reading to use the
book for such a purpose.

These books in no way seek to replace the standard
academic commentary to which I myself owe many important
insights. But they are the product of a slightly different
approach to the text. This approach, arising as it does out of
different presuppositions from those of many academic
commentators, sometimes forces one to come to different
conclusions from theirs about the origin and integrity of the
text, and the intention of the original author.

I have often been encouraged by pastors who have found
my books or lectures helpful in preparing their sermons.
These studies are written with a personal understanding of
this need for help in pulpit work.

RONALD S. WALLACE

ABRAHAM

Genesis 12—23

1
The New Beginning
GENESIS 11.31—12.3

The curse—and the grace of God

There is much to disturb us in the earlier chapters of the book of Genesis. We are told that a curse has blighted our environment (3.16–19). This is why we have to live with corruption, decay, death, with so much pain, with so much fearful distortion in the natural world around us in the struggle for existence. We are told that it is our sin that has caused the curse. We are born in it, we inevitably live with it and we cannot help ourselves out of it.

We are also shown some of those whom we have to recognize as our brothers and sisters. Their sin becomes worse as the story moves on from chapter to chapter, and as it becomes worse it seems to become more modern. Adam and Eve, proud, deceitful, drawn on by self-centred desire, give place to Cain. He murders his brother but afterwards at least hates having done so (4.8–13), and then, two generations later, Lamech appears. God has blessed this man in his family. He has been given three gifted sons, one musical, one artistic, one a technical genius—all inventive. They make the organ. They make the sword. Lamech, drunk, takes up the sword, finds fun in killing with it and sings a song about his exploits to the new music of the organ (4.19–24). Thus our human culture begins!

It does not make pleasant reading, and we ask: if it began this way may it not end this way? Man gone mad with all the gifts God has put at his disposal, finally destroying everything and everyone to the music that was meant to remind him of his maker and his eternal destiny.

But already, even before we reach our present chapter in this sober and dreadful prologue, there are things to give us hope. We can take some comfort in the fact that the curse was brought on by God himself—the loving God, entirely

1

free from malice or any evil passion, patient and wise and faithful. God not only allowed the curse to fall, he also decreed it. Therefore even the evil things we read of must be under his control. Moreover, his grace and goodness are active in the midst of all the human perversity. He puts a mark on Cain to prevent the worst that can happen from taking place (4.15). He endows the direct successors of this man with wonderful cultural gifts. He keeps his living contact with humanity by raising up people like Abel, Enoch, Seth and Noah, whom he inspires with faith. Therefore if our reading of these early chapters has disturbed us, it can also cheer us. When man fell, God decided to save. While he cursed 'the ground' (3.17) for a time, he did not curse the human race. He has decreed that life on earth shall never become hell on earth. He is going finally to send his Christ and his blessing!

The new beginning

The narrative suggests that God held everything in suspense for a long time. Things had to ripen, certain conditions had to prevail, a certain man had to appear before he began to intervene in human affairs in any final and decisive way.

The passage before us is the announcement that the time has come and that the man is there: *Now the Lord said to Abram, 'Go from your country and your kindred . . . to the land that I will show you. And I will make of you a great nation, and I will bless you . . . and by you all the families of the earth shall bless themselves'* (12.1–3). Everything from now on is to be different. The curse is to be replaced by the blessing.

This place in the Old Testament is very like that of the birth of Christ in the New. Can we not already hear the angels in heaven practising the chorus 'Glory to God in the highest . . . and on earth peace'? What God has begun in Abram is nothing short of the kingdom of God here on earth. It is the seed of a new age implanted at the heart of mankind. God has now intervened once for all in the history of the race, giving it a decisive turn and a new direction, so that now all man's despair can be turned into hope.

The Jews of a later generation, when they read this passage, interpreted the whole event as a new beginning of similar significance to their nation as that of the exodus from Egypt under Moses. Jesus himself often thought of his own mission as nothing more than the completion of what his heavenly Father had so wonderfully begun in Abram (cf. Luke 19.9; 13.16; Matt. 8.11). 'It is correct to say', comments Luther, 'that with Abram a new world and a new church began, for with Abram God begins once more to separate the church from all nations, and he adds a very clear promise concerning Christ who is to bless all nations.'

Yet it was a quiet affair! Nobody heard the great divine announcement but one man. All that took place on the surface of human affairs to show that God was beginning all this was the appearance on the far-too-crowded road of another uprooted family. No divinely printed placards were raised around them. No angelic choir appeared anywhere in heaven. Nothing registered on the surface of human events to merit even a local press report.

Those who study the history and archaeology of the area with which our story deals tell us that at this particular time numerous tribes or families not only occupied the land as settlers but roamed here and there through it following the great caravan routes. The arrival and departure of migrants was a feature of life in every community of that time. People were restless, living was hard. When they felt that things did not suit them in one place they went off to another, and sometimes they went out not knowing where they were going.

We are told at the end of chapter 11 that Terah, Abram's grandfather, had already made such a move when Abram himself was a child, from Ur of the Chaldees to Haran (11.31–2). Scholars inform us that such wandering peoples, who often made only a temporary settlement in different localities, were given the somewhat despised title of Habiri (or 'Hebrews'), and the fact that Abram was later known as Abram 'the Hebrew' implies that he was regarded as belonging to this class. It is tempting to adopt the suggestion made by one scholar that his forebears were involved in the

3

transport business of the day, i.e. in hiring out donkeys and drivers and other equipment along the routes, and that Abram himself took up the family occupation. Who could possibly have imagined that here, among the carts and the cash and the bargaining and the animal-breeding and the caravan-letting, God was beginning the work of glory that was to be fully revealed and completed in Jesus Christ?

It may be going on all around us today even though we see no spectacular signs of it—the blessing, moving on into the world's history to prevail over the curse! Abram is introduced to us here so that we can be delivered from all despair. The power that came into the world when he was called to his task is greater and more subtle than anything that insinuated itself into man's life when the serpent entered Paradise. The curse may have determined the past, but now it is the new Word of God that is to take over, control everything and decide destiny. The future belongs not to Cain nor to Lamech nor to the generation that rejected Noah, but to this lonely elect man to whom God spoke in Haran and to the Creator himself who has not gone back on his purpose of grace nor weakened in his power.

One man alone

God's plan involves the creation of a new community of mankind—of a 'nation' and a fellowship of 'all nations'. God himself is a community person. He is Three as well as One, and he loves to have before him in human life itself good and healthy community family and church life. The fall has isolated people, has turned individuals in on themselves, has created an insulating national self-interest, has made real world community impossible. Now through the blessing there is to be a drawing back of people into the original unity of mankind. The blessing will create this community which God loves.

The story of Terah's family migration from Ur of the Chaldees to Haran suggests that God tried to begin the blessing by calling a whole family unit. But Terah's family, as a collective group, obviously failed to reach even their

4

Canaan, the destination they had had in mind when they left Ur, and God had to begin again. This time he concentrated on convincing one man. Our attention now becomes focused entirely on the story of this single individual. God lingers over him and works with the greatest care over his relationship with himself. Several times we are told of the delight and satisfaction God finds in the response of this man alone (13.14 f,; 15.1 ff.; 18.17; 22.12).

This story of the God–Abram relationship is told with such significance and emphasis that we can never regard it as merely the example of a unique achievement in the history of God and man, a starting-point to be cancelled out once the glorious, world-embracing fellowship is consummated. What God's love expresses and achieves between himself and Abram is meant to be taken as typical of what he wants to achieve with each of his people. It is the real and joyful beginning of the final harvest of the blessing—a first-fruit complete and glorious in itself and the promise of a crop that will be universally the same.

Thus the blessing is launched out into the world in the context of a message that centres on the one individual as intensely as it does on the community. When God calls Abram, the message is not only, 'I want you as the founder of a new community!', it is also, 'I want you, for the sake of who you are and what I find in you, alone, before me.' God cares for the one as intensely as for the many and puts out all the energy and power he has to save the one, as well as to save the world, and 'all'. The Lord of hosts, the God of the Old Testament, remains always and is never ashamed to own the name of the 'God of Abraham and Isaac and of Jacob'. The saviour of mankind in the New Testament is the one who calls each of his own sheep by name (John 10.3).

For his own sake, too, Abram needed to experience this quite individual approach. He needed to hear his own name called by God. There in Ur or in Haran amid the mixed hordes of restless, purposeless people milling around in these crowded cities and trade routes, how could Abram ever have thought of himself as being of any significance in the

5

eyes of the creator of all things, or in the history of a world so crowded with people?

But the word announcing that all mankind was to be blessed instead of cursed comes to him, and as it comes it also says: 'You are not lost. You belong to me personally and dearly, and to my service and my kingdom, and I want to bless and use even you!' And now he begins to find himself treated as if he were at the centre of everything that matters! Now he begins to know who he is, and what life is for!

Throughout his whole career Abram continues to be thus strangely isolated before God, especially when God appears and speaks to him. Always, it is true, Sarai is there in the background, and sometimes at his side, for God does not loosen the ties that bind these two when he elects Abram. But the very closeness and inseparability of these two make it all the more remarkable that Abram should be so often called apart to meet with God. He is alone at the critical moment when the covenant is made. He is justified alone. He is alone in his responsibility of deciding before God when he is put to the final test on mount Moriah.

The shadow of a cross

We could think of several good reasons why, under his circumstances, God kept Abram so much to himself and by himself. Through such treatment Abram is made to feel all the more intensely God's personal demand for his whole loyalty and devotion. For under such conditions his attention cannot be diverted from God and the issues by discussion and debate with another.

But one special reason for Abram's increasingly intense isolation must have dominated all the others. The purpose God is beginning to work out with him is to find its climax in the coming of Jesus. Quite definite and unique thought-patterns and life patterns have to be developed throughout the history of the people who are to follow Abram. This unique understanding and these patterns will enable their successors finally to understand and appreciate the meaning of the life and work of the coming one.

One of the ways God prepared Israel for the coming of Jesus was to raise up from time to time during this long period of history lonely leaders and examples, mostly called prophets, whose sufferings and isolation foreshadowed the much more intense and ultimate sufferings of the coming one. Abram is himself the first of these prophets, and those who follow—for instance, Moses, Elijah, Hosea, Isaiah, Jeremiah, Ezekiel and others such as the suffering servant of whom we read in Isaiah 53—will look back to him as each in his own turn tries to fulfil the call of God.

Moreover, when he comes, Jesus too will recognize Abram as his forerunner in this respect, as one whose 'children' he is seeking to add to when he saves individuals like Zacchaeus (Luke 19.9) and as one who rejoiced, though afar off, to see his coming day (John 8.56–7). Jesus, too, in his loneliness will enter exactly the same school as was founded with Abram as its first pupil, learning 'obedience through what he suffered' (Heb. 5.8).

The immediate sacrifice

Before he even entered his career as a lonely pilgrim Abram had some costly decisions to make in suffering obedience to God. He had first of all to face having painful things said and thought about him by those whose respect he wanted to keep. He had to allow himself to become detached in mind and spirit from the local people. His growing experience of God, whose word he had to obey and to whose will he had to surrender, must have made him deeply critical of the common values and ways of thought around him. Long before he actually left Haran he had to begin to adopt a life-style radically different from that of his contemporaries. Thus there takes place through him not only a new beginning of God with mankind, but a new beginning of mankind with God.

The religious cults that had claimed his devotion proclaimed a god or gods cold, limited, distant, capricious—and now for Abram God had come near, warm, familiar, overwhelmingly strong, trustworthy, who spoke to people

7

he knew, who could be spoken to in response to his speaking, who cared about human ways and who was prepared to look after people who would take his way.

There was something so convincing in this new experience of communion with God, and in other signs that he had asked and received from him, that everything he had been taught to think about, and to worship around in his whole past religious tradition, even in his non-conformist family circle, was put into eclipse. In this aspect of his life beyond all others he had become a new man. There could be no mixing of the old religion with the new. The more he grew to understand the one who had come and called him, the more strongly did he recognize that he had to renounce the other totally. He had to go!

It was inevitable that many of those around him should in the end be glad to see him go, and should say so. They had felt for a long time that he was making himself superior, adopting a 'holier than thou' attitude. 'Noah', says the writer to the Hebrews, 'condemned the world' of his day (Heb. 11.7) when he began to live a different life from them all and prepared the ark for sailing away in. They laughed at him and cursed him too. Abram, by his new, rather lofty ideas and his 'superior' bearing, no less severely condemned the world of his day. If they cursed him, he had already been warned by God that they would do so (12.3).

The mounting tension therefore made the parting easier for some of his family and former friends. They were glad to be rid of the insufferable fellow! But Abram had a warm and friendly human nature and hated being misunderstood and rejected. The cost of the final break from the society in Haran is emphasized in the story: to leave 'your country' is hard, to leave 'your kindred' is harder; but when it comes to leaving 'your father's house' (12.1), Abram is touched where it hurts most. Von Rad says that to expect of ancient man such a breaking of ancestral ties was to expect 'almost the impossible'. Normally when tribes migrated they went together; Abram goes almost alone. He has, however, found one loyal friend, Lot; and Sarai his wife believes in him.

Abram and ourselves

Certainly we are not *all* meant to forsake our world as Abram did his, so that he could prepare, in his unique way, for the coming of Christ. God undoubtedly still calls some people apart specially to live lives of chastity and poverty and prayer for the rest of us. And most of us need to have such heroic examples around us. Most of us, however, have to stay and seek to share the new knowledge and life we have from God—the 'blessing'—with our neighbours and community. If we can do this effectively, as we are meant to, we are achieving something even more challenging and difficult than any cloistered saint can attain to.

Remaining as we are in this world, however, can we avoid being different in such a way that we will tend to be condemned? The world today is moving fast in the wrong direction. Even the moderately compromising Christian conscience will find itself unable to keep up with it. And when our conscience becomes really awakened by the Word of God we will find ourselves having to edge out of the mainstream in order to change our course. Our move is bound to be noticed, and interpreted as Abram's was. Jesus reminded us that in following him we might have to 'hate' 'father and mother and wife and children and brothers and sisters' (Luke 14.26).

The Sermon on the Mount begins with a radical description of a new way of life and a new attitude quite different from that dreamed of in any world in any age: 'Blessed are the poor in spirit . . . the meek . . . those who hunger and thirst for righteousness . . . the merciful . . . the pure in heart . . . the peacemakers.' Then it ends, as it was bound to end, with a word about the consequences of being different. 'Blessed are you when men revile you and persecute you . . .' (Matt. 5.1–11).

Can we avoid, therefore, to some extent being driven to God alone with a sense of inner detachment and perhaps a feeling of loneliness in the process? Certainly there is something unique in Abram's solitariness, for he was a pioneer in a way of faith that no one in history had ever been

9

on before. He had no saintly or heroic examples to set before him, whereas we have multitudes. But to watch him alone with his responsibility reminds us that there are times when the advice, leadership and support of others will be of no decisive help to us and we too will become isolated in the decision we have to make before God—a decision whether it is to be God or mammon we serve; whether it is to be Christ and his gospel or the present world with its vain desires and false ambitions that is to become the dominant influence in our mind and heart. When we face such a crisis we cannot be other than alone.

We may ask if Abram could have been the leader and pioneer he was, and could have given God the response he required, had he not been so much alone with him. Perhaps this is where we fail so badly today. We too often wait for someone else, especially the pastor, to give a lead on a matter that has been on our mind and conscience and in which God is waiting for us by ourselves to take a lead. And of course the Church suffers for lack of that solitary bit of leadership! Revival does not come because, though people want it, everyone is waiting for it to start with someone else.

2
Moving on under the Word of God
GENESIS 12.4–9

Seven promises to one command!

When God commanded Abram to get out of Haran, he gave him at the same time the will and strength to do so. This is implied in the phrase: *So Abram went, as the Lord had told him* (v. 4). Because the Lord spoke, Abram was able to break the ties that bound him where he was and to rise also out of his inner bondage. When God commands men or women to do anything, he effects what he commands. This simple fact is illustrated for us from the beginning to the end of Holy Scripture. 'God said, "Let there be light"; and there was light' (Gen. 1.3). It is illustrated time and again in the biblical narrative. 'Sarah your wife shall have a son . . . The Lord visited Sarah as he had said, and the Lord did to Sarah as he had promised' (18.10;21.1). The whole story of Israel as it is told in the historical books continually brings out the point that God's word when he speaks it by seer or prophet never returns void, but accomplishes what God promises and prospers in what he has sent it to do (Isa. 55.11). But it is especially in Jesus' own ministry that we see it happen. 'Jesus said "Follow me." . . . And he rose and followed him' (Mark 2.14). 'And he said to the man who had the withered hand . . . "Stretch out your hand." He stretched it out, and his hand was restored' (Mark 3.3–5). So it began to happen with Abram. God said and Abram went.

Yet we must not imagine his obedience to the word of God to have been the response of one of our modern gadgets, set automatically in motion or direction from a distant push-button. Nor are we to think of his response as an act of blind and forced servility towards some incomprehensible order, overwhelming him in fear and constraining him against his own will and intelligence.

The phrase, *So Abram went, as the Lord told him*, implies some conscious understanding of the kind of way he had to go and of the kind of plan he was involved in. Abram has thought it out, as he has decided and obeyed. Moreover, his assent is given gladly as well as fully. He hears seven promises piled one on top of the other (12.1–3) and only one command! Obviously the command to 'go' is simply the logical outcome of all these promises. It is the inspiration of the promises and the joy of privilege that move him. When God himself has a vision and a plan for human history, and wants men and women in it, he prefers to have them working with full understanding and joyful co-operation, rather than playing the role of blind, blunt instruments or ignorant tools. 'Surely the Lord God does nothing', said Amos, 'without revealing his secret to his servants the prophets' (Amos 3.7).

Jesus told his disciples that the kind of response he wanted of them was not that of the 'servant' who does not know what his master is doing but that of the 'friend' who has been fully briefed and consulted and who understands his master's purpose, as Jesus himself understood God's purpose for himself (John 15.14–15). Therefore we are meant to hear Jesus promising far more often than commanding, warning or rebuking. The Sermon on the Mount begins with the beatitudes ('Blessed are the poor in spirit . . . Blessed are those who mourn . . .') and goes through nine of them (Matt 5.1–10). As we read them through we can turn them into a series of new commandments by Jesus, and we can hold these qualities before us as ideals we must attain in order to achieve the promised blessedness. But these very beatitudes, like the Old Testament text before us, are primarily a series of promises. They are the announcement of the gifts which Jesus himself has come to give us and which he is appealing to us to receive from his hand.

'I will make of you a great nation' (v. 2) is the central promise which God makes to Abram among the seven. Abram could not possibly have made anything of himself! His own human life lived as our pattern of obedience was a Yes to the promises of God (cf. 2 Cor. 1.20). And of course the New Testament itself is designed to show us the Person in whom all the promises are so fulfilled that we can make them ours in making him ours.

In the seven promises many important details are missing. There is as yet no indication which 'land' it is to be and no promise of a 'son' to Abram and Sarai. But now, even at this early stage, as he moves on one of the details becomes clearer. God stops him and says to him, 'You are now in the heart of the very land I am going to give you and yours', and it will not be very long before he is shown the full extent of this land, its limits and borders.

As we follow him in the later chapters we will see this process of clarification carried further. Only gradually does it begin to dawn on him that it is to be through one of his own sons that this great nation is to proceed from him. Then it is made clear that Sarai and no other is to be the mother of the child. The destiny of his nation, the kind of worship and devotion God requires, gradually become more clearly outlined.

Abram's certainty, too, grows as the promises become clarified, and as he moves on to higher and deeper levels of understanding what God's will for him actually is in concrete terms. Of course he lapses at times into despair and then recovers. There are low points and high points, but the main level of assurance tends to become higher all the time. In the text before us we see this process going on.

When he arrives in Canaan the first place he halts is in the area of Shechem. Here the deeply rooted and established paganism of the land showed its most arrogant and strongest face. *At that time the Canaanites were in the land*, writes the narrator (v. 6). How can this puny and strange individual ever hope to change all this? It is a low point. Abram had not thought it would be like this and he has to struggle with unbelief.

But at that moment when it appeared impossible, the Lord speaks to the baffled, half-doubting arrival. *To your descendants I will give this land* (v. 7). The word transforms him. His response is unhesitating and triumphant. He erects his altar within full sight of the entrenched forces of darkness, as if to raise a flag in the face of all the brutally opposing facts of the situation, and claims the whole place for God. 'It was a sign', says Von Rad, 'at first still non-combatant—of infinite significance.'

It is significant, too, that his first journey is a circular tour of the then beleaguered territory. After going north to Shechem, he travels south, pitches his tent between Bethel and Ai and then moves on towards the Negeb. Commentators find difficulty in understanding why these details of his first journey seem to matter in the narrative. Calvin considers that God's purpose in making Abram do this was 'to teach him self-denial', but Cassuto rightly notes that later in the history when Jacob returned from his exile to possess the land, he too started at Shechem, went to Bethel and then

13

moved towards Hebron. Likewise when Joshua began the conquest of the land it was exactly along this stretch of territory that he started his possession of the land. We have to interpret Abram's journey as an ideal conquest of the land in the name of the Lord. He is declaring: 'One day this shall belong to me.' No doubt this journey is also a declaration of defiance to those who are now in possession.

Abram did not know when he started out how 'impossible' would sometimes appear the difficulties in the way of the fulfilment of the promises. Especially would this be so when he heard that his old and barren wife was to expect her child. But his certainty would actually grow even when he was put to this test.

> He did not weaken in faith when he considered his own body . . . or . . . the barrenness of Sarah's womb. No distrust made him waver concerning the promise of God, but he grew strong in his faith as he gave glory to God, fully convinced that God was able to do what he had promised (Rom. 4.19–21).

A familiar situation

It is not difficult to feel ourselves into Abram's experience and struggle here. The commands and promises of the Bible certainly put us increasingly to the test—if we will read them. 'This is your land—claim it in my name!' It comes to us this way especially when we read words like Paul's 'all things are yours . . . whether . . . the world or life or death or the present or the future' (1 Cor. 3.21) or when we read in the book of Revelation: 'The kingdom of the world has become the kingdom of our Lord and of his Christ' (11.15); or when we read even about ourselves: 'the law of the Spirit of life in Christ Jesus has set me free from the law of sin and death' (Rom. 8.2). We discover, as we move through the New Testament, that the claims of Jesus become more specific, extend more and more over what we once thought deeply private and personal and embrace ever-expanding spheres of family, social and international life.

It all seems ridiculous, for the Canaanite is too deeply entrenched for the land ever to belong to Abram! Yet as we face the challenge to believe, we are thrown back—as was Abram—on listening again to the promises of the Word. These will let us neither rest nor despair, for the book is filled with detailed and vivid descriptions of the new possibilities opened up for people in Jesus Christ and his gospel. It tells us deliberately and often that our evil ways can be corrected, our hearts can become purged of self-centredness, love can become real rather than phoney. It speaks about the Spirit of God being able to transform relationships within the home and family and even to mend marriages. It speaks of the gospel also as a power great enough to transform societies. It began to speak this way with Abram.

The building of the altar

Soon we read of the building of another altar (v. 8) and then of a movement back again to the altar he had already built (13.4). This building and re-visiting of altars seems to indicate something of significance in the life both of Abram and of his successors.

We ourselves tend to think of altars primarily as places of offering and sacrifice. Cain and Abel must have built them in order to make their offerings to God (Gen. 4). Noah built one for this purpose (Gen. 8.20). 'You shall build an altar to the Lord your God of unhewn stones; and you shall offer burnt offerings on it to the Lord your God' (Deut. 27.6)—so ran the Law. They seem to have been places where the worshipper dedicated himself or herself to God as well as the sacrifice.

But we are told that at Shechem the Lord *appeared to Abram* and spoke (v. 7). This is the first time ever we read of the appearances of God to Abram that were later a marked feature of his life with God, and we can believe that the altar was built significantly on the first place such an event occurred, to mark it as the place of a vision which inspired new self-commitment to God and brought a fresh intensity to his faith. At the second altar between Bethel and Ai he *called on the name of the Lord* (v. 8). This phrase indicates that there he had found and there he expected to find the presence of God with him in a specially real and close way as he called on him, and we are justified in thinking that this altar also marked a place as originally significant as the altar at Shechem. Abram, then, built altars where God had 'appeared' and where it was believed he could be invoked to come and give his presence and his fellowship. In this custom he was followed by Isaac his son and by Jacob his grandson (35.1; 46.1–2). Canaan became to him not only the land of the promise, but also the land of the altars.

Therefore instead of thinking of altars as being only places of sacrifice we are to think of them rather as places of sacrament—places where the vision of and communion with God was restored. We are justified in thinking that the Patriarchs built them at the command of God, and that God himself also promised to make them special meeting places between himself and those who would come to them and offer their worship and make their offering and prayer. We are therefore not far astray in thinking of the altar as taking the same place in the life and worship of Abram and his immediate successors as the sacramental worship of the Church takes in our life today. We are not so superstitious as to imagine that God is simply there automatically as we go through our sacramental ritual, but we know that where he gives a promise to come and bless us, and we with trembling, seeking faith respond and call on his name, we will not find that he disappoints us.

Commentators sometimes read the order of things here as being of some significance. The first thing Abram did in Canaan was to build an altar, and only then do we read that *he pitched his tent* (vv. 7–8).

God—the first and the last!—always with priority over our own concerns, and always to be represented by something built to stand for ever. Abram, in deliberate contrast, is content to live in what is flimsy and transitory. If we followed his example, even a little, we might have much stronger churches, a much better equipped ministry and much more efficient relief agencies.

3
Schooling in Self-Discovery
GENESIS 12.10–20

Out of depth

How strong we can become when we live by the grace of God! Our characters can change, and it can become as if we were indeed completely born again. But however much we have progressed, if we begin to become presumptuous, over-confident, careless, forgetful of God's grace, how quickly we are forced to discover again that we are still simply human. 'I am nothing, if not a man', confessed St Francis de Sales, after years of sincere effort to become also a Christian. Abram, too, has to make this discovery—that he is still the old Abram.

He has certainly begun to discover a new side of himself now that he is beginning to know God—the side we come to know by looking upwards. If at any stage in his life he has asked himself the questions, 'Who am I?' and 'What is life for?' he now needs to ask them no more. He knows himself as one called by name, cared for personally by God and caught up into his service. He has begun to share the 'blessing' of which we too know something when we know Christ. To know himself as one made and destined to enjoy and share all this with others like himself before such a God is answer enough to all his ultimate self-questioning. Need we ourselves ever ask for any more than this?

But now God has to teach Abram to know himself again by looking *downwards*. He must begin again to discover how weak, empty and untrue he can become out of this new and

17

close relationship with the living God. God therefore allows him to go down to Egypt for a few months and to drift away from the land of the promise and the altars.

Suddenly we see him struggling. He is out of his depth. He becomes excited and afraid about his safety. He puts Sarai's life and honour at risk to save his skin. He tells a lie and tells her to tell it, and he soon finds himself in the kind of mess that any stupid book-keeper or politician can get into when dishonesty is practised. There is an attempt at cover-up to save the situation. When Abram says of Sarai, *She is my sister* (v. 19), it is a half-truth, for she is in fact his step-sister. When Abram by this claim implies 'She is not my wife', it is a very serious falsehood. The half-truth covers the big lie! Who would have believed that Abram could be in himself such a weak fool? The situation has become too big and complicated for him to deal with or even to grasp in all its issues. This is Abram's downfall.

As we read through the whole narrative of the God–Abram relationship and watch how easily Abram falls when he is tempted, how unwise he can become when he is perplexed, we will recognize that he is made simply of the ordinary stuff of human life. He had been an idolator before he was called (Josh. 24.14) and did what was done by pagan men in the service of idols. His election to be the father-founder of God's new community was an act of pure grace. God does not wait till he has found the man suitable for his task— tough, heroic, wise, loving, outstanding in mental and moral qualities. Only one thing makes Abram outstanding: he is 'merely the material that the divine majesty seizes through the Word and forms into a new human being and into a patriarch' (Luther).

Out of touch

The story itself indicates in a subtle way that Abram himself is responsible for what happens. We can compare what is said in verse 4, *Abram went, as the Lord had told him,* with what is said in verse 10 in our present context: *Now there was a famine in the land. So Abram went down to Egypt.* In the earlier section Abram is led by the word of God. He is always listening and looking. He moves from altar to altar. But in the present section he is driven into the sad venture in Egypt by hunger and the need to survive, then he is driven round by fear, then he is driven out by rebuke and shame. In the whole section that deals with the incident in Egypt there is no mention of any word of God or any vision of God coming to Abram himself while he is there. From day to day instead of moving from altar to altar he moves from expedient to expedient. He allows himself to drift.

The most serious aspect of the matter is that he has drifted out of touch with the living God himself. Abram is not out of the hands of God or out of the plans of God, when he is in Egypt. God still protects him by afflicting Pharaoh (v. 17). He even shows signs of favour by making him wealthy (v. 16). But the heart of what it means to be blessed by God is lacking—the presence, the close friendship, the living communion, the personal touch, the clarity of a shared vision of the promised glorious future. Indeed, all those things that he found so real at the place of the altar—they are now gone.

And so our religion can become second-hand religion. Someone else brings us the message he has heard from God, but we never hear it for ourselves. The intimacy, the warmth, the personal devotion, the enthusiasm—they are all gone from us, and all we have left is a relationship, formal, distant and at its best correct. 'We salute but we do not speak', was Voltaire's explanation to a friend who asked him why he went to the length of taking off his hat when a religious procession passed him by in the streets of Paris. 'You have left your first love', was the very pointed accusation and warning which Jesus sent in his message to the church at Ephesus (Rev. 2.4), where devotion to him had once been so full of vitality and sparkle! Here is where we can sometimes find ourselves with Abram.

But Abram feels it and longs to be out of it! 'Where is the blessedness I knew when first I saw the Lord?' It is a sign of how deeply he regrets what has happened to him that on his return to Canaan his first act is to go to 'the place where he had made an altar at the first' (13.4), in order to call 'on the name of the Lord'. He wants things back as they had been between himself and God. He knows exactly where the root of the trouble lies.

The grace of God in the far country

Where was God and what was he doing when Abram drifted to Egypt? During a period of long and nauseating temptation, Catherine of Siena found her mind assailed with every form of evil suggestion, which she resisted much better than Abram did his. After it was over, ashamed, she asked: 'Where wert thou my sweet Lord, when my heart was so full of such great darkness and bitterness?' And God replied, 'I was within thy heart my daughter'. He told Catherine that the reason why she had found no pleasure but only sadness and bitterness in the guilty thoughts that had assailed her was due only to his own presence within her—all the time she had thought him absent!

The present narrative shows us God present with Abram, even though the man has drifted himself 'out of touch'. Though this is a story of Abram's weakness, it is also no less a story of God's grace and power. He lavishes patience. Never in the whole sad affair is Abram verbally and directly rebuked by God for what he did. It is indirectly, through the words of Pharaoh, that God gently but surely leaves a sting in Abram's conscience (vv. 18–19). The humbling lesson is taught through gentle chastisement (cf. Heb. 12.6) rather than through severe punishment. God's gentleness worked. The lesson was never forgotten, and the pupil never again strayed in this particular way.

Abram's own attitude of heart is decisive, too; when he felt driven out of the land by the famine, he did not attempt in any way to retrace his steps to Haran, where he knew he would have found help. Basically his heart is bent on following and obeying God's will.

Moreover, he gives ample proof to God of his repentance as the intricacies and wretchedness of the affair begin to catch up with him. This is why God can deal so gently. This man is changing. Something in him now wants above everything else to learn what God has to teach him and to receive what God has to give him. Even though he feels so far from God, he longs for God. When he arrives back, he immediately hurries to the altar, as the Psalmist hurried to the temple. 'O God thou art my God, I seek thee, my soul thirsts for thee; my flesh faints for thee, as in a dry and weary land where no water is' (Ps. 63.1). He wants things back to what they had been like in the beginning. He wants to experience renewed assurance and vision. He wants God to lift him out of his muddledness. He wants forgiveness and restoration. It is a plea to God to break his silence, and the tone of the subsequent narrative leaves us in no doubt that his expectations are fulfilled.

The discovery of the boundary lines

Abram discovers that in Egypt he had been out of bounds as well as out of touch and out of his depth. The contrast between his whole experience of Egypt and what he finds as he returns to the altar teaches him that he can remain certain of God's presence and of his continual personal guidance only by remaining within the boundaries of this one land he has been promised. It was his journey beyond such boundaries which had proved disastrous, had taken him into uncertainty and caused him to lose his touch. He comes back obviously convinced that it must become a rule for himself and for his immediate successors only to seek the fulfilment of the promise within this land. Never again will he himself move out of it, and on his death-bed he will extract an oath from his servant that Isaac himself will at all costs be kept from moving outside what is now his homeland (24.6).

This remarkable story stands here, therefore, to warn Abram's successors that to journey outside this land as their founding father did could become for those who serve the promise only a way into repeated confusion and uncertainty. But those who followed him in the faith had to rediscover this truth all over again for themselves. For though their later journey into Egypt under Joseph was made under what was at the time a gracious dispensation of providence, nevertheless the attempt to settle down in Egypt ended in disaster and bitterness. When they finally regained their homeland after years of wandering in the wilderness they began to have to discover all over again the truth that what God had in store for their future would be revealed and worked out only within the confines of the place he had so graciously given them and led them into.

Relevance within contrast

How clearly, at this point, does the New Testament contrast with the Old. Jesus' final command was to 'go therefore and make disciples of all nations' (Matt. 28.19). The Good Shepherd now seeks to lead his sheep out into the world and 'goes before them' to be with them everywhere (John 10.4). We dare not draw bounds either geographically or socially or nationally in our programme of Christian evangelism. We dare not now erect fences within any sphere of the world's politics or industry or culture or commerce and say, 'Beyond this the Christian faith has no relevance!' For us there are no boundaries to our mission.

But as with Abram in Egypt so for us in the world of today, often we become confused and uncertain. Sometimes we have no clear guidance as to what is right and what is wrong, or even as to what is best for the furtherance of the gospel. Anyone who is familiar with the ethical discussion that takes place among Christians as to the rights and wrongs of the decisions people have to make today in the conduct of government and finance, in medical practice, in solving marital difficulties, in guiding the young, in balancing the good of future generations against the urgent needs of today, in the distribution of the world's resources, will know that the answers are never simple nor agreed. What those who approach a problem from one side feel to be right, those who approach it from another side feel to be quite wrong. In Abram's time the king of Egypt proved he had more insight and better judgement than the patriarch, so in modern times the world sometimes knows much better than the Church how to guide its affairs with rectitude, for God does not leave it without some light by which to make ethical judgements, and books on ethics by Christian theologians are sometimes as poor and naive as Abram was in Egypt. If we look carefully again at this strange story we will find the patriarch with his moral confusion very close to us.

This does not mean that we do not go on our mission into this world without our certainties and confidence and joyful message. The ethical confusion in which Abram found himself in Egypt did not alter the certainty he had about the promises of God and the real purpose of human life, which no one knew but himself. And if, as Luther insisted, Abram went about preaching, his ethical confusion did not destroy the essentials of his message, though it did hamper his immediate effectiveness.

It is of importance to us still that as we go out into the world, the way back to the altar is always there open to us and inviting our return. In the same part of Jesus' teaching in which he describes himself as a shepherd who leads or brings out his sheep (John 10.4), he also describes himself as the door by which the sheep 'go in and out' to find pasture (John 10.9). There must be for us that which corresponds to Abram's return to Bethel again to call on the Lord and seek his presence. If we 'go out' following him, we must also come back to him from where he went out. Too many Christians, intent on stressing the outward direction of the church's service, especially its international and social mission, fail to concern themselves also with the need for a continual return inward—for the pilgrimage back with Abram to the altar of renewal and vision. The result is that ultimately they lose their bearings, become confused in their motivation and wane in the moral and spiritual resources necessary to maintain personal commitment.

If God worked this all out for Abram, so quietly, graciously and powerfully, we can take heart. When we too are situated as Abram was, forced to make decisions in areas where our vision is necessarily limited, forced to journey in ways that seem to lead us beyond the range of any clear or definite word from God about the muddled issues that face us, then we can trust him still to be with us, over us, near us as we make our tentative judgement and seek his blessing for the plans we have to make. We are neither condemned nor forsaken nor put beyond the range of his detailed and intimate overruling guidance.

We need not deny ourselves today the recovery of certainty and strength that Abram found in his day. The Word of God has been spoken once for all in Jesus Christ, in his life and teaching, in his death and resurrection. It illuminates for us around itself a large enough region of moral certainty, of unshakable truth, of firm assurance, to enable us always to regain our sense of purpose, our will to start again, to correct our former false decisions and to make better judgement in the future—and along with the word he gives us his renewing presence, comfort and power.

A footnote on other interpretations

This story, more than any other in our series except that of the sacrifice of Isaac, has produced widely differing interpretations by commentators, and in fairness to the reader who may wish to be informed of these, we indicate some.

Most commentators, as we do, read the story as a warning about how quickly and easily the servants of God, even at the moment when they seem genuinely established in their faith and devotion to God, can fall into serious sin. One accuses Abram of shamefully abandoning his wife to the lust of a foreign potentate for material gain. Calvin, more gently, accuses him of folly and unreasonable caution. Luther, who always tends to whitewash the patriarchs, justifies Abram here and consistently interprets the story as an illustration of his sanctity; though he certainly sinned 'to some extent' a 'sin of weakness', he was wise to be suspicious of the Egyptians, merely followed the dictates of prudential reason and in no way failed in faith or discarded it. His lies avoided harm to others, and if suffering was caused it was not Abram's fault. Cassuto believes that Abram was not blameless, but looks on the incident as being allowed to happen so that in the person of Abram there might be acted out a kind of prelude to the later deliverance of Israel from Egypt.

Certainly the story does remind us that God can and does act ruthlessly to fulfil his promises.

Some of the more modern commentators are firm in the conviction that the book of Genesis consists largely of a collection of folk-tales current in different areas of the ancient world, originally connected but given fresh shape and context in the area in which they circulated, and later gathered together by the editors of the sacred writings for arrangement in some historical sequence, without much concern, however, to produce any kind of exact history. It is held that this particular story is of the kind that a primitive audience would love to hear told for their entertainment—the story of the tricky man and the beautiful woman and the unsuspecting ruler. It could in the telling be elaborated on with all kinds of details according to the taste and mood of the audience. Somehow it became attached to the name of Abram. One version of it found its place here in the Abram tradition; another version of it found its place at a later point (cf ch. 20). A third version of it was attached to the name of Isaac (26.6–11), and therefore we have the same story appearing a third time in the book of Genesis. The story itself is judged by them to be rather pointless, its preservation being mainly due to its entertainment value.

The fact that this kind of story actually occurs three times, however, can be taken simply to indicate that each recurrence is to be regarded as significant and requiring careful attention, rather than as trivial. It also means that we have to take especially careful note of the differences in the situations and happenings in each story, for we can assume that the writers of the Bible were not in the habit of indulging in unnecessary repetition. If there is apparent repetition we can assume there is some extra meaning to be brought out in the narrative. We ourselves do not find it strange that a man should fall twice in similar circumstances—or that a son should follow a father, even in his faults!

4

Abram and Lot

GENESIS 13.1–18

The undermining of a friendship

Several times in the Bible we are reminded of the strengthening and enriching effect of a friendship. We think, of course, of David and Jonathan, Paul and Barnabas. We can think, too, of what the friendship of his disciples meant in the life of our Lord. It is in the book of Proverbs that we are reminded that finding such a friend is even better than having a blood relation, for 'a friend loves at all times' (Prov. 17.17) and there is one 'who sticks closer than a brother' (Prov. 18.24). It had been something like this between Abram and Lot. Their friendship had had the greater meaning and value because it had had its roots in a common faith and hope, deeply shared, in the promise. Lot is mentioned even before Sarai, in the list of those who accompanied Abram from Haran. What this friendship meant to Abram we see reflected in his concern here to keep it intact (vv. 8–10) and in his later efforts in battle and in prayer to save his nephew from disaster (14.14, 18.23 ff., 19.29).

But human friendships, in the Bible, never involve the same close and life-long covenant as does marriage, and as working partnerships they tend to break up. That between Paul and Barnabas was broken up through misunderstanding. The harsh circumstances of life terminated the effectiveness of that between David and Jonathan. And now we find the same kind of thing happening between Abram and Lot. It is tragic that in this particular case the cause of the break-up is an alienation that has its roots deep down in the realm of belief. Lot is beginning to lose his faith.

The deepening of the tension

The visit to Egypt obviously did not help. Perhaps when Lot found Abram so weakly stooping to what could be interpreted as underhand dealing, he may have begun to have doubts about the basic integrity of his old associate, and this would give him an easily-found pretext for deciding finally to go off on his own. It was, however, the astonishing growth in the wealth of each man that brought the issues to a head.

After their return, quarrels began between their herdsmen. *Their possessions were so great that they could not dwell together, and there was strife between the herdsmen* (vv. 6–7). Wealth in cattle was cumbersome. It involved the need for space, the careful choice of location for grazing. It meant that the areas they could move to within the land were more limited. Tension and even strife now begin to arise at points where there have been none before. Between these two men who had been so close together when there seemed to be less to lose, there now have to be more rules, more formality, more distance—in case they should fight. The possession of wealth is beginning to show its tendency to divide, isolate and embitter.

But the possession of wealth has also raised questions and brought temptations which each answers in a different way. Egypt was much richer and more highly cultured than Canaan. Even Abram must have felt some temptation to settle there, or at least to set up some base for business and exchange. But his pilgrimage to the altar at Bethel has helped him to settle again with God for a life committed totally to the fulfilment of the promise. With Lot, however, the Egyptian routine upset everything. It was the kind of world he felt he could really fit into. He liked especially the glimpses he had got, and the stories he had heard, of the ways of life of the free cities such as Sodom and Gomorrah. He is becoming convinced that the most real things in life are those that can be counted and evaluated over counters or on shop floors or in market places. He is beginning to lose his zest for life lived round one of his uncle's altars.

The two are now facing the kind of question which their successors in Israel will have to face all through their history as they consider their own heritage after centuries of obedience to the word of God, and look round on the richer and more powerful nations who outshine them so much in earthly glory. Had their fathers really been on the right track? Was the past justified—the toil of their leaders and forerunners, the agony of the prophets, the faithfulness of one generation to another in handing on the pure tradition, the centuries of endurance at the price of so much sacrifice? What kind of wealth is it worthwhile deciding to seek in this life? It was the question squarely put to the people when they were in exile in Babylon and tempted by the local wealth and opportunities to settle down among the idols and ideals of the Babylonians: 'Why do you spend your money for that which is not bread, and your labour for that which does not satisfy?' (Isa. 55.2). When all the time God was offering them another kind of 'good' and satisfaction. To remain a true child of Abram meant that though wealth was possible it could never be a first consideration in choosing a way of life and that the true way sometimes must lead to the choice of poverty.

Jesus was frank about it to his disciples. At the time when 'many turned back and walked no more with him', he turned to his disciples and said, 'Do you also wish to go away?' (John 6.67). He was deliberately putting them into tension and forcing them to make a fresh decision about him now that the first stock-taking had made some of the difficulties of the business quite clear.

The concern of Abram

Sensibly Abram faces the situation. The break has to come. Lot must leave the homestead. Yet surely the parting can take place under the guidance of God himself, with gratitude and affection on both sides. When the quarrels break out between his herdsmen and those of Lot he is concerned for the reputation and even the safety of the family. *At that time the Canaanites and the Perizzites dwelt in the land* (v. 7). This meant danger if they quarrelled openly, and in any case the genuineness of their beliefs and purposes could be called in question if they were not seen to live at peace with each other.

But his more enduring concern is about what is happening inwardly and secretly to Lot himself. Till this man in the end finally and irrevocably makes his decision to choose the way to self-destruction, Abram leaves no argument unspoken and no appeal unuttered that could change his mind. Lot must not go backwards in mind and heart to the wealth-idolatry he renounced when he left Haran. He must remain in the land of promise and play his part with Abram in shaping the destiny of the people of God, finding his source of inspiration and guidance at the altar of the Presence.

It is always with deep pathos that the Bible shows us people, sometimes prominent like King Saul, or of lesser importance like Orpah (Ruth 1.14–15), who start off well in the service of God and then turn back. It is a tragic and absurd thing that some seem to choose from the start to have nothing to do with God and his kingdom. It is even more tragic and absurd that some can 'taste the powers of the world to come' and then commit apostasy (Heb. 6.6). Lot was the first to court this danger, and Abram was the first witness of such a tragedy. We can share Abram's concern when it happens around us today. It was shared by Jesus when he saw the rich young ruler whom he had looked on and loved turn away from him sorrowful because his possessions prevented him from entering the kingdom of God (Mark 10.21–2). It was shared by Paul when Demas forsook him, having loved 'this present world' (2 Tim. 4.10).

From altar to hill-top

The narrative implies that when the final decision was made, the two men had moved from the altar at Bethel to a standpoint which gave both of them a wide view of the promised land and which therefore would probably be situated on a hill-top nearby.

From the altar to the hill-top! It may have meant only a

very short climb, but the change of view is significant. At the altar Abram has had the opportunity of fresh insight—into the love and wisdom, the tenderness and faithfulness, the openness of heart and mind, of the God who has brought him thus far and had never failed him. At the hill-top he is to be given a new panoramic and symbolic view of the whole range, wealth and fullness of the earthly inheritance and historic future God has promised to his descendants in this land to which he has returned. He is told at the end of the day to stand there in the centre of it and look all round. *Lift up your eyes, and look from the place where you are, northward and southward and eastward and westward; for all the land which you see I will give to you and to your descendants for ever. I will make your descendants as the dust of the earth; so that if one can count the dust of the earth, your descendants also can be counted. Arise, walk through the length and breadth of the land, for I will give it to you* (vv. 14–17).

No one could ask for more. Now he can see that simply by remaining faithful to the word of God in the place God has called him to and provided for him, he has more to satisfy and challenge him than anyone could desire. Why had he ever thought of flight to Egypt from this?

The altar and the hill-top still remain for us distinctive and complementary viewpoints at which we can take our stance when we want to renew our dedication to the service of Christ and our devotion to him. Viewing the gospel from the altar means trying to look within it at the heart of the mystery. It means, for example, reading of how Jesus himself in his intimate dealings with men and women must have appeared to those who gave their lives to him in personal love. It means looking again at the cross, with the strange power it has to open up our hearts to the mystery of God's forgiving love for individual sinners and of God's vindication of righteousness and holiness in bringing his love to us. It means looking again at the eternal love and knowledge which the Father shares with the Son and the Son with the Father in the Holy Spirit and trying to realize that our destiny is to share that! It means coming again in penitence to the Lord's Supper where Jesus himself seeks to meet us in order to show us, and make more real to us, the mystery of the union by which he dwells in and with flesh and blood. It is by looking at this point of vision that we are brought most simply to the renewal of our dedication, for 'the love of Christ' seen in this way 'controls us, because we are convinced that one has died for all; therefore all have died' (2 Cor. 5.14).

But we can also be brought to the renewal of our devotion and dedication by viewing the gospel, as it were, from the hill-top. This means looking again at what it has done for mankind, at what it can offer and accomplish in the world today, at the range of its promises and the greatness of its power of salvation in every sphere in which it is really allowed to penetrate and revolutionize. It means looking again at the degree to which it towers above every kind of 'religion' or 'ethic' or 'ism'. It means looking again at the history of the Church in order to see how in spite of the ever-recurring failures and follies of men and women in his service, God has never failed to work out his purposes and to prove himself trustworthy.

The appeal to look and the refusal to see

The whole land therefore now lies before Lot as a witness— to the truth of the promises on which he has built his life with Abram, to the ample wealth that he will not be denied if he continues in the service of the promise and, indeed, to the greater and more glorious eternal things to which God is seeking to lead him. Abram appeals to him to look at it all— to consider, to choose and to stay. *Is not the whole land before you? Separate yourself from me. If you take the left hand, then I will go to the right; or if you take the right hand, then I will go to the left* (v. 9).

Lot lifted up his eyes, says the narrative, but all that he sees is all that he intends to see: nothing less and nothing more than the place he has already chosen before he looked, *and saw that the Jordan valley was well watered everywhere like the garden of the Lord, like the land of Egypt, in the direction of Zoar; this was before the Lord destroyed Sodom and Gomorrah*

(v. 10). It is in fact a refusal to see. He looks only on the fringe of what he is asked to gaze at, and then his eyes drift to what is beyond—and he chooses only what he allows within the sphere of his vision. He makes his choice by refusing to look.

The appeal is again and again repeated throughout the Bible. When God's people were tired, disappointed and tempted to revert to false gods and choose other ways, the prophets constantly appealed to them to open their minds to what God had already done and to what he was doing and to count their blessings. When Jesus saw his disciples, too, worried by unbelief because they were tired, and tired because they were worried by unbelief, he said 'consider'—a word which simply means 'look', and he pointed to how the lilies are clothed so wonderfully by the Father who cares much more for his human children (Matt. 6.28). To a congregation who had started off well in the Christian life and were now becoming faint-hearted under persecution and tempted to compromise, the Apostle uses the same kind of word but points to Jesus himself: 'consider Jesus . . . consider him . . .' (Heb. 3.1; 12.3). The appeal is always to look so that we can see.

But strangely, as with Lot, often people refuse to take even the simple first steps of looking. Israel, complained Hosea, were 'bent on turning away' from him (Hos. 11.7), and in Jeremiah's day Judah 'turned their back to him and not their face' (Jer. 2.27). They refused stability and chose vanity, refused wealth and chose poverty, refused forgiveness and chose condemnation, refused liberty and chose bondage, simply because they would not even look.

What explanation could there possibly be for the fact that when 'He came to his own, his own people received him not' (John 1.11) except that they were unwilling honestly to look either at what he was in himself or at what his worth was in the sight of God or at what he could do for them?

The diverging paths and the ever-widening gulf

Each man seems to become confirmed in the opposite attitude he has taken and to become more and more drawn into what he has chosen, and as the distance widens it becomes more and more clear how far they are from each other in heart and mind. *Thus they separated from each other* (v. 11).

Abram moved his tent towards Hebron and there *built an altar* (v.18). He is now confirmed in his devotion. It is no more even a possibility that this man should ever again desire to choose any other service or any other source of gain or comfort in preference to living, as he has been doing, by the word and grace of God. Any further test to come can now be only of the extent to which he is able to go in yielding what God asks for.

Lot's journey in the direction he has chosen is described as if it were rapid: *Lot journeyed east* (v. 11), Lot *dwelt among the cities of the valley and moved his tent as far as Sodom. Now the men of Sodom were wicked* (vv. 12–13). In the next chapter we read that Lot dwelt in Sodom (14.12). Later we find that he built a house there and betrothed his daughters to its men!

It must be noted that though they separate so decisively and move themselves so widely apart from each other, there always remains something that seems to bind them together, though it is almost unbearably strained. The New Testament calls Lot 'just Lot' (2 Pet. 2.7), and it seems that even to the end of his life he retained something of his faith and struggled to give it expression when the issues around him became acutely challenging. Abram on his part never lost his concern for Lot.

We can find a clue to what made these men so different in the fact that each had an entirely different view of how the greatest gifts of God and life are meant to be gained and kept. We are meant at the beginning to notice the magnanimous generosity of Abram in giving Lot first choice when it had to be decided where each was to settle. *Let there be no strife between you and me . . . for we are kinsmen . . . if you will take the left hand then I will go to the right; or if you will take the right hand then I will go to the left* (v. 8). What concerns him first is the maintenance of good personal relationships between kinsmen and, if possible, the keeping of Lot in the promised land. He makes this very generous gesture with perfect spontaneity and ease. He carries his wealth in an open hand before God. He is willing to have it less or more as God decides either to take it from him or to keep it with him.

Lot loses exactly what he sought so avidly to possess and hold on to, while Abram, free from any anxiety about his possessions, receives more and more from the hand of God. We recognize a touch of irony in the next chapter when we read that the first thing that happened to Lot when he arrived in Sodom was to be taken prisoner and to lose everything. He was possessed by what he so eagerly sought to possess.

We truly possess only that from which we are detached and about which we have no anxiety. Such detachment comes only as the by-product of a whole-hearted concern to seek first the Kingdom of God.

5

Abram in the Power Struggle

GENESIS 14.1–24

The inevitable war

This story begins with an impressively detailed account of an ancient war. The nine participating kings are all carefully named. We are told of how they formed their alliances, *four kings against five* (v. 9), of the routes taken by their armies, and that the exact year it happened was *the fourteenth year of Chedorlaomer* king of Elam (v. 5). There is so much appar-

ently irrelevant detail in the whole first part of this chapter
that Luther says it seems to be 'altogether barren' and
admits that he cannot understand why Moses is 'very prolix
in his description of the time and the place'. Yet the insertion
of all these details does seem for the first time to put Abram
in an exact historical setting. Surely one day we will find out
who at least one of these kings was, when exactly he lived,
and thus date Abram too. But though archaeological findings
have indicated that the geographical details of the story are
more accurate than critics used to think, research has so far
been unable to verify or contradict the historical details or to
help us with dates.

It is inevitable, however, that Abram should at some time
be involved in war. Moreover it could become an important
matter for his successors to know how he fared and what
attitude he took when the war swept across his threshold.
Would he resist—or submit to the pressure of the enemy?
Could he expect divine help and guidance even in such an
enterprise? The generations who followed him and lived by
the tradition he helped to establish were bound themselves
to become frequently involved in international alliances and
battles. They would themselves be tempted to take part in
the intrigues of one king against another. As they too faced
battle they would become anxious about the possibility of
survival, about the questions of policy and alliances. This
incident in the life of Abram would become important to
them as they faced the questions raised by such involvement.

Token success

Abram's effort to rescue his nephew Lot from his captors
met with considerable success, but we must not exaggerate
the extent of his prowess or achievement. Lot's allies are
referred to with some contempt: there seems to be a touch
of scorn in the reference in verse 8 to their foolhardy
pretensions and a note of ridicule in their being caught in
the slimy pits. Lot had poor allies and it did not take much
skill or power to capture him in the first place.

Abram, however, is obviously very brave and loyal. He

35

enters sensible alliances, and though he can muster only three hundred men or so of his own he succeeds in an outstanding way, and for a moment he is shown as a military hero. The writer, however, probably intends us to understand Abram's victory more as a miracle than as an act of military skill or genius. This is the forerunner of many another such victory in the history of Israel when God takes the control of battles into his own hands, gives insight and courage to some, brings fear into the hearts of others and stupidity into the minds of others, so that in the end the battle is won by the few rather than by the many. The God of Abram proves himself the 'Lord of Hosts'. Abram's preservation and success in delivering Lot are signs that in the midst of the world power-struggle the people of the promise can rely on him.

Temptation and rescue

Now Abram has to face all the temptations of success in the service of God—the temptation of being given a 'good press', of a growing reputation among all kinds of people. Even the wicked now want to fête him and share their spoils with him. He is the local hero.

Though it is obviously only a token success, there is danger in the sheer joy and achievement he feels in the victory itself. Is he beginning to think that possibly God intends him or his descendants after all to become part of the world's power structure? Now Abram himself needs help, fresh vision and a recall to sanity.

The help comes in an extraordinary and divine intervention in which God himself dramatically brings a change in Abram's mind and thoughts. Just as the king of Sodom is approaching him to offer him his share of the spoils, and no doubt to arrange future alliances, one of the most strange and puzzling figures ever to be described in the pages of the Bible suddenly appears: his name is Melchizedek. He seems to have had some local importance in the region and a fairly widespread reputation in his day, and the story calls him *the king of Salem* (v. 18). If 'Salem' is meant to stand for a place, it could denote a very old Canaanite shrine, but of course the word also means 'peace'. Melchizedek's title is *priest of God Most High* (v. 18), whom he himself calls also *maker of heaven and earth* (v. 19).

What this intervention does for Abram is remarkable. In contrast to the loot which the king of Sodom is about to foist upon him, Melchizedek brings him a simple serving of *bread and wine* (v. 18) from the hand of God. It is a challenge to him to open his mind afresh to the fact that it is better to receive a modest portion from the most worthy giver than any amount of wealth won in a conquest involving human blood and brutality—expecially if it is given by the hands of one like the king of Sodom! In contrast to the plaudits showered upon him in his moment of triumph, Melchizedek obliges him to attribute his preservation and success solely to the 'God most High'. As a warning against any idea he may have picked up about the possibility of great achievement for men through war, he seeks to raise Abram's thoughts to a kingdom of peace, founded and furthered only by pacific means.

Abram's encounter with Melchizedek should be regarded on the same level as the other extraordinary visions and encounters with God experienced by leaders and prophets in Israel's history at turning-points in their lives. In the presence of the king of Salem and Peace, Abram makes a pledge that alters immediately his whole attitude and his approach to the king of Sodom. *I have sworn to the Lord God Most High, maker of heaven and earth that I would not take a thread or a sandal-thong or anything that is yours, lest you should say, 'I have made Abram rich'* (v. 22–4).

All this suggests that there were already within one of the local traditions in Canaan the beginnings of an elevated conception of deity. Indeed, it suggests that even before he brought Abram out of Haran into these Canaanite surroundings God was making preparations to help him as he struggled to understand his destiny and that God had either left for him or cultivated for him there at least a dim point of light in the darkness of its paganism.

The fact that this priest-king appears as if from nowhere

and then disappears as suddenly, that we have no previous or later reference to him in the story of Abram, that he speaks and acts with such sheer majesty and mystery caused later biblical writers to regard him as someone of quite extraordinary origin and ordination. In the Epistle to the Hebrews it is affirmed that his appearance and ministry to Abram at this juncture were expressly designed to represent and foreshadow the ministry that Christ would fulfil when he finally appeared among men. It is also suggested in the same epistle that Christ himself was present in and behind the Melchizedek intervention, as he was present in other unique Old Testament visitations and visions, speaking to and dealing with Abram personally, just as he speaks with and deals with us today (cf Heb. 5.5–10; 7.1–22).

The kingdom of God and the power struggle

This incident is a help towards an answer to the question: how far does the fulfilment of God's kingdom depend on participation by the people of God in the power struggles of this world? We cannot evade the fact that Abram did allow himself to become actively involved in this struggle. For this he had two main reasons: first, the stability of life in his area seems to have been in some way threatened. Naturally a man 'rich in cattle' could hardly avoid joining in any collective steps that were taken for the protection of family and flocks. He seems to have entered into a defensive alliance, and he has a band of his own trained men. Abram's second reason for becoming involved is the fact that Lot his friend and nephew has been taken prisoner with all his goods through the invasion of Sodom following a battle fought *in the valley of Siddim* (vv. 8, 12, 14).

No suggestion can be made therefore that Abram had any other decisive motive than those of maintaining law and order, humanity and justice, and security of home and country. He may have argued to himself, also, that unless these things were protected then the promise of God could never be fulfilled in the course of history. But he does not enter this war simply because he sees it as a useful means of furthering the promises of God.

But in the end he retires from the war a very half-hearted, indeed a half-ashamed soldier. In the previous chapter it became clear that Abram's descendants cannot fulfil their purpose unless they refuse to grasp after wealth or to immerse themselves in the surrounding pagan culture. In this chapter it becomes clear that they must equally avoid becoming caught up in the struggle for security and power based on military strength. At the moment Abram receives the bread and wine from Melchizedek, he begins to realize as never before that the fulfilment of his destiny is not to be dependent on his cultivating the arts of war. Neither he nor his successors need ever become serious contenders for world power. The king of the rescued nation approaches him at the end of the battle in order to make him a king too! But then Abram is suddenly rescued and given a new vision of the bigger and more urgent business he should be about—and the upshot is that never again do we see him attempting to play the part of a man of war. His is not this kind of power.

Involvement and separation

This chapter seems to confirm the impression given throughout the whole narrative so far that Abram is a man strangely aloof from the world's affairs, always maintaining a distance between himself (and especially his family circle) and the surrounding people. He feels that this is how God has called him to live. Yet when he finds himself really needed he has no hesitation in giving himself, his skill and loyalty, and in risking his life. He does all this with complete freedom, withholding nothing so that the common enterprise may be a success. At the end of the affair he withdraws himself as speedily as he had involved himself at the beginning and returns to his strange aloofness.

It is precisely because Abram is so separate that he can become free in his involvement, and he is careful ultimately to maintain his freedom within his involvement. With Lot there is a complete contrast. Lot's decision is to avoid the kind of separation he dislikes in Abram, to mix freely with others, to involve himself as far as he can in the common interests and pursuits of everyone around. But the result is strange and paradoxical. Lot, in losing his power to remain separate, loses his freedom to become involved. He becomes submerged. For him in this affair involvement becomes merely the helpless acquiescence of a victim carried along wherever the tide of the world's life flows or ebbs, with no power to influence affairs or to give one chirp of witness to the reality of a living God. All this is Lot's fate because he refuses to remain separate. The writer of the story is deliberately seeking to underline the contrast between the two men in this respect.

We too have to learn what it means to become 'involved' without losing the freedom to be what God intended for us when he called us to become different in order to be his witnesses. Jesus himself was totally involved with the struggles and temptations and sufferings of mankind. But he was also as totally free, holy and separate as he was totally involved. Abram is a much better pattern for us than is Lot when we are thinking out the form our obedience to God should take today.

The vow to maintain his honour

Abram's reply to the king of Sodom is noteworthy. It expresses spontaneous disgust at the very thought of participating on such a low level with such a low-minded man. In receiving from Melchizedek he has been a guest at the table of the most High God. He has received bread and blessing and fellowship from one whose presence raises everything to a new level. How can he now seriously share with the one who ruled life in Sodom? His life has received a new ethical direction and dynamic as a result of the blessing of God.

Already he has faced the king of Sodom and expressed his loathing of what he stands for; Abram has thought this out carefully, made a deep basic principle and uttered a vow about it: *I have sworn* (v. 23). Decision on a matter like this is not to be left to his changeable feelings; it is to become a rational principle of his behaviour that he cannot take what is devoted to God and yield it to perverted use; that he cannot in his behaviour give the lie to everything his new relationship with God is meant to bring into being in his life.

Of course the passage brings us right into the atmosphere and teaching of the New Testament. Indeed it brings us to the Lord's table. We too have a dignity and honour to think about that will affect our ethical conduct. There is not the least doubt that we are taught there that there are things we cannot do, gains we cannot accept, careers we cannot adopt, pleasures we cannot seek, fellowship we cannot enter, dirt we cannot handle whether it clings to money or literature or forms of amusement—all because we have received a new status and dignity by becoming sons of God and experienced a new and intimate fellowship with the eternal son of God who has given his life and made us his members. We, too, have to make our ethical behaviour a matter of rational commitment to the services of God. We cannot leave our ethical behaviour on important matters to be arbitrarily decided, now one way, now another, as our moods change. There is enough consistency in the nature of God, in the nature of our relationship with him, in the nature of life and humanity and sin to be able to draw some lines and make some definite vows of commitment for the way of life we are to choose to follow.

So before God, as he takes the bread and wine from the hands of this strange priest-king, Abram makes his vow. His giving of a tenth of everything to Melchizedek, whatever this implies, is at least a sign of the depth and reality of this new commitment and of the completeness of his rescue from falsehood and compromise.

6

The Assurance and the Covenant

GENESIS 15.1–21

The challenge to complain

Abram feels like complaining. His disappointment over Lot has been a long, hard trial; the news of his nephew's imprisonment came as a shock. Then there was the rescue operation, the exciting victory and the sudden switch of feeling when Melchizedek intervened. Abram has been tensed up—only to give way to a depressing reaction. Perhaps the experience of a war so near to his homestead has made him nervous about the future safety of his family.

Moreover, things have gone badly behind the home front. The mention of Eliezer of Damascus (v. 2), his chief steward, is made in such a way as to imply that Abram has found him tiresome and difficult. This man was bound to inherit Abram's estate and name unless his master had a son of his own as his heir. Could God really mean such a slave and a foreigner to inherit the promises for the sake of which he, Abram, had sacrificed everything?

But he has tended to bottle it all up inside. Possibly he thinks God would not like to hear his protests and complaints. In any case there is something quite selfish in his grudging attitude to Eliezer. And he feels a bit ashamed that he is in such depression. But God encourages Abram, even challenges him to voice his complaint, and shows he likes to have frankness and openness before himself on the part of his people. This is why he approaches Abram with words that he knows will touch him precisely where he is hurting. *Fear not*, he said, *I am your shield; your reward shall be very great* (v. 1). The words '. . . shield . . . reward' are linked with thoughts that God knows to be present at that moment in Abram's mind, and they challenge him to talk about his anxieties.

Sometimes, instead of dealing openly with God, we repress

in an unhealthy way what we feel, relegating it to the unconscious part of our lives where it festers and brings serious restraints into our lives and our relations with others. God knows that only a free, full and honest expression or even an eruption of our thoughts and feelings can create the conditions for a true relationship with himself and a restoration to personal health. So he tries to touch us gently and sharply at exactly the place where we are damaged in this way. This is why the Bible is so full of words addressed directly to people burdened under every kind of perverse or pathetic human mood, in the hope that they will begin to talk back frankly and end the play acting with him.

The challenge to believe

Abram is called to believe as well as to complain. *Fear not, Abram. I am your shield; your reward shall be very great* (v. 1). God wants frankness and complaint only as the accompaniment and expression of a basic faith in him. Even in their bitterest and most desperate expression, the cries of complaint and lament that we have in the Bible as our examples are always those of men and women who in their lowest ebb believed in the God to whom they were crying out: 'I believe, help my unbelief!' (Mark 9.24).

What God says to Abram in the introduction to this chapter is the most warm-hearted and tender word that he has so far heard from God. He is called by his first name, by a voice that he knows has never so far said anything false to him. In God's assurance that all will be well at the very points about which he is most bitter, Abram is definitely promised the protection and the encouragement he has thought himself deprived of. 'Abram, look straight at Me, again, and look now, for I am what you really need most!' *I am your shield . . . and . . . reward* (v. 1).

It is this last point on which we require to dwell for a moment. The challenge is to Abram to lift his attention from what is promised to the Promiser himself. He has no doubt become too fully absorbed in some of the details of God's promises and is judging God himself by the extent to which in his own judgement he has found these already fulfilled. The kind of grudging thoughts that come to his mind are revealed in his question: *What wilt thou give me?* (v. 2). God, knowing such thoughts before they were uttered, says: 'Am I not enough at the moment?' Perhaps it is significant of a growing maturity in the relationship between God and Abram that up till now God seems to have emphasized the what and the how—what he was going to do for the world, what he was going to give to Abram, how he was going to bless. But now he begins to say, *I am!* (v. 7).

And of course it reminds us of how Jesus always ultimately thrust himself into the centre of everything he did, every appeal he made and every picture he painted of the future. He seems to be doing it today. 'I am . . . the truth' (John 14.6), he says to those who are tending to become so immersed in theological thoughts that they cannot see his face. 'I am the light' (John 8.12), he says to those who want to find God and the meaning of life and are looking everywhere else. 'I am the life' (John 14.6), he seems to be always saying to us in our search for adventure, excitement and personal freedom. 'I am the true vine' (John 15.1), he seems always to be saying to those who are so concerned today about the roots from which they have sprung and the class of people to whom they belong. 'I am the bread of life' (John 6.35), he seems always to be saying to those who believe that all that really matters is the gold we can spend and the food we can eat. 'I am the resurrection' (John 11.25), he seems always to be saying to those who are neglecting the opportunity and joy of a new life here and now with him, because they are over-absorbed in speculation about the end of the world and life after death. 'Come to me and rest and drink and live.' This shift of focus from the things given to the One who gives began centuries ago, with God's word to Abram.

The moment of confession

Abram releases all his pent-up feelings and pours out his complaint and concern: *O Lord God, what wilt thou give me, for I continue childless, and the heir to my house is Eliezer of Damascus? . . . Behold thou hast given me no offspring; and a slave born in my house will be my heir'* (vv. 2–3).

We ourselves have to learn today to 'cast our burden on the Lord' (Ps. 55.22), especially if it is a burden of pent-up inner repression. After Jesus met the woman at the well in Samaria, he soon discovered that she was hiding too much guilt within herself. And it was he who switched the conversation so that she was directly touched and challenged precisely at the point of her need; and when it was all brought into the open and she became free under the light of his grace, she ran back to her village with news about him that simply expressed her sense of glorious relief: 'Come, see a man who told me all that ever I did. Can this be the Christ?' (John 4.16–29). In her case she herself had said little and done little. Jesus himself entirely on his own initiative brought all the hidden, uncomfortable truth to the light without even asking her about herself.

But to most of us God gives a longer time to think it all out and to find ourselves, and to express it all ourselves in his presence. We can find ourselves as we really are if we begin to take more seriously the fact that God has given us the Bible to help us to open up in his presence. As we read it we find it full of psalms, songs, laments, cries of despair, complaint and confession, from people who discovered to their joy and relief that God loved to listen, wanted to hear such complaints and desired that in his relationship with his people they should be free to hide nothing from him. All this helps us to understand what must be at the heart of all our prayer, which is nothing less than a pouring out of the heart 'into the bosom of God himself', as Calvin used to say. This is Abram's discovery, and it is the beginning of a new level of friendship and frankness in his relationship with God.

It is to be noted about Abram's outburst, however, that as

he utters it, it turns out to be a confession rather than a complaint. Any sting in the ears of God it was meant to have was lost in the utterance. When the presence of God begins to be something really felt by us, and we seriously think about who he is, what he has done and what we ourselves are we find ourselves with no ground to stand on in order to justify any accusation against him. Then we are at the place where even the best saints have found they could only say, 'Lord have mercy upon me!' God is too faithful and good for us to keep up the pretence that we could ever be let down by one like this. He is too holy for us to stand and face up to him.

A reproach and a sign

There is a note of reproach and self-defence on the part of God. Why should Abram imagine even for one moment that in the hands of God he would be subjected to such trials, asked to give so much, encouraged to such definite and fervent beliefs, only in the end to find all his natural, tender hopes about his future brutally crushed—as if God were playing a joke in such a matter of life and death! *This man shall not be your heir; your own son shall be your heir* (v. 4).

And now God suddenly makes the stars confirm his word. Certainly they were already shining clearly and impressively; perhaps Abram has already noticed that it was a glorious night. But when God tells him to look, they take on new meaning as signs of his faithfulness and power. *Look toward heaven, and number the stars, if you are able to number them . . . So shall your descendants be* (v. 5).

So that night the stars speak of God, as he speaks of them, and God uses them in his speaking. And they also illustrate the Word, and Abram becomes the stronger in his faith. How varied are the things God told the people and prophets of the Old Testament to look at when he wanted to give signs and illustrations of the truth of his word! The variety has been endless. Sometimes he has used great miracles, sometimes trivial ones (Exod. 14.19 ff., 2 Kings 6.3 ff.); sometimes he has used thunder in the heavens, sometimes fire on earth (1 Sam. 7.10, Exod. 3.1 ff.); sometimes he has used natural objects such as the twig of an almond tree (Jer. 1.11); sometimes industrial objects such as the clay on the potter's wheel (Jer. 18.1 ff.); sometimes domestic objects such as a boiling pot on a fire (Jer. 1.13). Regularly, too, in Old Testament times he used the objects and ceremonies prescribed for the temple ritual of sacrifice and worship especially at Jerusalem.

Today, since Christ has come, we know that some of these old ceremonies have been abolished. The one sacrifice has cancelled out the need for the multitude of bloody ones. And with such a clear and convincing Word as we have in Christ crucified and risen from the dead, we do not need any constant repetition of what was formerly so prominent. Therefore God asks us to look at what we do in the Lord's Supper, and Baptism. How eloquent these simple things— the bread, the wine, the water—become as God speaks to us about them, tells us to look and uses them in his speaking!

The moment of justification

And now comes what is so far undoubtedly the greatest moment in Abram's life. His faith, at least for this moment, becomes perfectly oriented, and his response is so wholehearted that God rejoices and feels honoured. Abram *believed the Lord; and he reckoned it to him as righteousness* (v. 6). At this moment, in solemn resolve he accepts God himself and God alone as his reward and shield, and every trace of anxiety to possess anything other than God vanishes. His heart leaps to God like the psalmist's: 'Whom have I in heaven but thee? And there is nothing upon earth that I desire beside thee' (Ps. 73.25).

Now it becomes clear that it is not the promise Abram is clinging to, nor his newly illustrated destiny, nor the fulfilment of his career of faith and obedience, nor his own faith, but God himself. 'We do not say', comments Calvin 'that Abram was justified because he laid hold of a single word concerning the offspring . . . but because he embraced God as his Father.'

This openness of Abram before God, his unreserved personal trust, his willingness to commit the future into God's hands and relax with him because he is good—this is what shows God that Abram is in a right relationship with himself. The writer of the story at this point, taking an analogy from the law courts, says that God 'reckoned' Abram's faith-relationship to himself 'as righteousness'. God is here likened to a judge, faced with a man in the dock against whom there are countless justifiable charges, but in the scale of values held by the Judge, and in the ends pursued by his love, no other consideration can stand for a moment beside this one great and thrilling fact: that the man is basically in a right relationship to the One whose verdict alone has any ultimate validity. The future between Abram and God is now completely decided. As a famous Jewish commentator puts it: 'He trusts in God who replies, I shall remember this.'

So this is all God wants from us, an open, frank look at him as we see him in Christ, a full and free acceptance of his promise to be himself our reward, friend and salvation, and an abandonment of every support we might have had to any self-righteousness.

The giving of the covenant

And now, for Abram's sake, God gives expression to the new stability and clarity that has come into his relationship with Abram by entering a covenant with him. When men in those days wanted to make agreements with each other, they often went through a simple ceremony. They would kill an animal, cut it in pieces, lay these on the ground in two rows so that the parties to the covenant could walk between them without touching them. When the two parties made this walk, it was a sign that they were calling for the fate of the animal to come upon themselves if ever they broke their vows to each other.

God makes Abram kill several animals, lay out their parts and keep watch over the scene, warding off attacking birds of prey throughout the day till he is weary and sleepy, and dreams. And *When the sun had gone down and it was dark, behold a smoking fire pot and a flaming torch passed between these pieces* (v. 17). It is the second sign given that day to Abram. It is God—the God who will later reveal himself at Sinai in smoking fire—passing between these two parts of the sacrifice, and thus pledging himself in a covenant with his servant and his descendants. At this stage God alone enters the covenant. Abram's time to respond will come. God first of all binds himself and pledges himself to Abram before he asks Abram to make his own pledge in response. It is God's way to love us before we respond to him, to be there before we turn to him and to be listening before we speak. It is out of pure grace that we too can make our covenants with him and pledge ourselves in response.

The covenant is entered simply because God's love is unchangeable in its ways and is never confined to the whim or mood of any limited moment or space of time. If God's love is to find any true expression at all it inevitably involves the setting up of some sign of its constancy and reliability. It is always 'for better, for worse; for richer, for poorer'. The covenant is therefore given to assure Abram himself that the love he has responded to has a never-changing foundation and can always be relied upon to express itself in regular and orderly ways. It provides the kind of framework in which the kind of love God has and gives can best be expressed. An Old Testament scholar, Norman H. Snaith, distinguishes between two types of love in the Old Testament. 'Electing love', he says, 'is sometimes inexplicable because purely emotional—a love that leads one to select this person rather than that . . . But "covenant love" or "steadfast love" though it has warm emotional overtones has stern duty as its essence.' It is 'shot through with a sense of loyalty and obligation' and 'is entirely dependable beyond all whim and caprice'. By enclosing Abram within a covenant relationship with himself God assures him that this love will never vary and that it will be the basis and norm of all his dealings with him and his descendants for ever.

49

The dread of great darkness

Before he finally lets Abram go God repeats, for the third time at least, the promise of *this land* (v. 7), and in answer to the question of how its fulfilment is to be brought about (v. 8), Abram seems to have been put into a kind of dream-state, given a very strange vision and told a very strange story. The atmosphere grows heavy, Abram is shown for the first time a dark and forbidding shadow cast over the way in which his descendants are to travel in the service of God. A fearful and prolonged period of suffering is to come upon them. As Abram is told of it he himself is subjected to what is called *a dread and great darkness* (v. 12). It is as if in mind and heart he himself is being called to share beforehand in simply a small foretaste of the coming sorrows.

The prophecy about the future is made during the giving of the covenant. As Abram is looking at the parts of the slaughtered animals lying there in blood and is engaged in chasing away the birds of prey that are trying to devour them (v. 7), the dread and darkness come upon him. Both Calvin and Luther believed that the slaughter and dismemberment of the animals was meant to signify to Abram's mind the kind of affliction that would come upon his posterity, and that the birds of prey were meant to stand as omens and signs of the enemies of God who would always be there in the background ready to devour his people. Therefore for the first time it was conveyed to Abram that this people of the promise, around whose history and future he had built so much of his hope, would be a suffering people and would go through periods of slavery, exile and the deepest humiliation in order that the promise might be fulfilled.

Abram must have been deeply disturbed in all his settled thinking as he opens his mind to what is being told him. It is merciful that he is put in a deep sleep as it comes to him and that he is thus relieved of the full pain and shock. Up till now everything said to him has indicated that his posterity will be 'blessed' and 'a blessing'. Now for the first time he has to understand that to be blessed by God in this world can mean being plunged into dereliction and deep humiliation. Moreover he begins to understand that to be a 'blessing' to others can mean taking judgement on oneself. But in the midst of all this humiliation and judgement, the people of God will be upheld and vindicated. The nations that refuse to give them peace and freedom will not themselves prosper. The nation that holds them in captivity will be itself crushed and forced to yield to God's will (v. 14). The 'Amorites' (the term includes all the inhabitants of the land of Canaan who are to be displaced by the people of God) will be allowed to live on undisturbed till their 'iniquity' is 'complete' (v. 16) or ripe for God's judgement, and then they will be displaced. Thus the broad picture of the future is given. No more details are drawn.

We can best interpret what all this means in the light of the gospel. Israel in responding to the call to become a blessing to all nations had to become the people among whom a suffering Messiah was to be received, nurtured and let loose on the world. But a nation destined to bring to birth a suffering Messiah had to be a people who understood within its own life in a measure and with an insight unique among all nations something of the meaning of the vicarious suffering they were to recognize as they looked at him. To teach even one nation that in order to redeem mankind it was God's will that one should suffer on behalf of many, that the righteous should suffer on behalf of the guilty, was a long process of education, not simply by centuries of teaching but by centuries of experience under the hand of God. This nation had to become poor in order that others might be made rich; it had to suffer judgement in order that others might be set free. Its education in these things now began with Abram.

7

The Hagar Affair

GENESIS 16.1–16

All flesh is grass

Luther is not at his best in his interpretation of this incident. He suggests that everything done by Sarai and Abram, the two saintly spouses, was done in good faith and only after months, even years, of prayerful thought and earnest discussion, and in hope of the mercy of God. The proposal involved heroic self-denial on the part of Sarai and was carried out with heroic self-control on the part of Abram. They were both mistaken in the course they took, but it was a very pardonable and natural mistakenness. The mischief that resulted from the whole affair was caused by the devil himself, who can work the same havoc in all well-ordered family, state or Church affairs. Moreover, when their mistake became obvious both of them showed fitting signs of repentance.

Surely we are nearer the mark if we interpret this story of Abram as a warning to us rather than as an example. After his experience in the previous chapter, this kind of faithlessness and folly should have been impossible on his part. The whole story here helps us to understand why, in a later century, one who claimed Abram as his father in the faith also wrote, 'All flesh is grass and all its beauty is like the flower of the field. The grass withers, the flower fades' (Isa. 40.6–7). And the change takes place so soon—'goodness . . . like the morning dew!' (Hos. 6.4). This chapter warns us that, at these very times when we feel most justified, we can do others most deadly and damaging wrongs and remain untroubled in conscience about it.

The failure and folly of the faithful

For Abram and Sarai, obedience at this stage in their lives means waiting upon God. But they have grown desperate and refuse to wait. They persuade themselves that they have to do something to bring about the fulfilment of what God has promised: *Behold now, the Lord has prevented me from bearing children; go into my maid; it may be that I shall obtain children by her* (v. 2). Sarai's suggestion to Abram could not be regarded in those days as morally wrong. Barrenness in a woman created very deep sorrow and carried some reproach with it—and it must have caused even deeper sorrow, and not a little mystification, to this couple who had by now been led confidently to expect offspring under the promise of God. Sarai's proposal is simply to take the clever and accepted legal way out of all the difficulty. A barren woman could get what she could claim as a child of her own if the husband's child by the maid was born, as it were, 'on the knees of the wife', so that it came symbolically from the womb of the wife (Von Rad).

In trying to produce the fulfilment of God's promises they resort to a method that really lacks straightforwardness, that enables them to evade the real difficulties of the situation and that produces a solution that is too clever, shrewd and original. Having ceased to seek the full fulfilment of the promise in the best possible way, they substitute what is merely a second-best fulfilment on a much lower plane and pretend to themselves for a short time that they are by this means going to produce the real thing.

'Under three things the earth trembles', says the book of Proverbs, 'under four it cannot bear up: a slave when he becomes a king, and a fool when he is filled with food; an unloved woman when she gets a husband, and a maid when she succeeds to be mistress' (Prov. 30.21–3). Anyone in Abram's day should have known this, either from current traditional talk or from experience of life itself. Proverbs exactly similar to these circulated everywhere even in Abram's time, and there were laws in contemporary codes allowing for the discipline and correction of female slaves under exactly such circumstances. But with Abram and Sarai their folly was the only wisdom they would listen to, and when we are in a mood like this true wisdom is bound to seem like folly, and even God has sometimes to allow us to prove ourselves fools through our mistakes (1 Cor. 1.25–9).

The faithfulness of God

Now we have to take note of the patience and faithfulness of God towards Abram and Sarai in the midst of the results of all this folly. For everything they did in their perversity God takes responsibility. In the end, when the situation they have created has become one of almost irrevocable, comfortless and harsh tragedy, he intervenes, alters radically the immediate situation and keeps it from ever yielding its worst fruits of bitterness and guilt. Hagar is saved from death. Abram and Sarai are saved from culpable homicide and the way is opened up for a fresh start.

Moreover, it was obviously never God's intention that Abram should become the father of the child Ishmael. Yet God takes serious and continuing responsibility for the little one who has now been so patently stigmatized as a human 'mistake' or 'accident'. So fully does God take responsibility that he gives to the child of Hagar promises that are linked to those given to Abram and yet allow for the natural make-up and bent of the child growing in the womb of such a mother. Hagar's child is destined to have an important place in the providential ordering of human history. He and his successors are to turn out to be the very difficult and extreme brand of non-conformists who will present a healthy problem to over-confident social and international planners. They are to have the unpredictable qualities of the wild ass—untameable and unmanageable as he roams the desert, refusing to settle down to normality. Ishmael is going to help to keep established nations in health and to limit their over-ambitious expansion by continually creating insoluble borderline problems and healthy diversions from too much 'progress'.

The idea that God is willing to take responsibility for

bringing such good out of our follies and mistakes certainly has its dangers if we take it as a fact for granted and live carelessly assuming that since all will come well in the end, the decisions we ourselves make do not matter very much. We dare not assume that God will cover up for us always as he did for Abram and Sarai. His decision to help Abram and Sarai out of their mess was an act of sheer grace, and we sin very seriously against his love when we say, 'Let us do evil that good may come' (Rom. 3.8). But to those who in fear and trembling seek to avoid such presumption, and nevertheless fall into the same areas of confusion as trapped and held Sarai, it is wonderful news that still today God can work in the same gracious way and make 'all things' (including our tragic errors in judgement and their sometimes fearful consequences) to 'work for good to them that love God' (Rom. 8.28).

Where sin abounded—grace much more

Nowhere in the narrative is the triumph of grace in the midst of human sin more clearly illustrated than in what happens with Hagar herself after she has been forced to flee from home. *The angel of the Lord found her* (v. 7). Abram and Sarai have certainly lost her, but God is there with his angel, and in his angel. It is characteristic of the God of the Bible to want to be there, especially with the outcasts and victims of human sin. The blind man in the Gospel story was cured by Jesus, and when the Pharisees persecuted him and cast him out because he professed belief in the healer, and even when his own parents stood aloof from him, 'Jesus heard that they had cast him out, and . . . found him' (John 9.35). The contrast between human love which always in the last resort proves weak and resourceless, and God's own love, is brought out time and again in the Bible. 'For my father and mother have forsaken me, but the Lord will take me up' (Ps. 27.10).

'Can a woman forget her sucking child that she should have no compassion on the son of her womb? Even these may forget. Yet I will not forget you' (Isa. 49.15). This finding of Hagar by God is not the result of her seeking or her prayer. She is found because the divine shepherd does all the seeking.

The conversation with the angel helps Hagar to see her human situation in a clearer and calmer light and to come to a sensible, practical decision about what it is best to do. *Hagar, maid of Sarai, where have you come from and where are you going?* (v. 8). She has to learn that through her flight she is evading the only way into a tolerable and viable future that is open to her. Her only hope at this stage in her trouble and her destiny lies alongside Abram and Sarai, sharing her situation with them however difficult some aspects of it may be; there is no other alternative. Has she really thought out whether even the slavery imposed on her by Sarai is not better than death for herself and her child? If she had been able to suggest one alternative other than death, possibly she would have been allowed or encouraged to take it. But there is none, and God makes her return to slavery tolerable by giving her hope of ultimate freedom when her child grows towards manhood.

Many commentators read the question of the angel as if it was primarily intended to help Hagar to understand that she was doing wrong in running away—a tactful encouragement to confession and a gentle warning against going on strike! Others find in the words of the angel an attempt to lead Hagar in to the path of self-knowledge—as if it were a primitive form of the question, 'Who am I?' Certainly at least she must have come to some measure of understanding of her own guilt in the presence of the Angel of the Lord. Such encounters with divine visitors nearly always brought a sense of sin to those who had them. Hagar's reply, 'I am fleeing from my mistress Sarai', sounds like a confession of guilt. She must know that her own involvement in the whole sorry affair is not blameless and that her secret flight is illegal. But the main purpose of the angel's question is to raise the common-sense issues and to begin to edge her gently back home for the sake of her own and her child's future.

What is much more important in the experience, however,

is what Hagar learns about God and about the destiny he has for both herself and her child. She comes away from the place with a new name for God: *She called the name of the Lord who spoke to her by the name 'El Roi'* (v. 13 NEB). What this title actually means is very much disputed by scholars. Most of them think that it expressed something of her wonder in the 'seeing' or oversight of God over both the details of her present circumstance and the future—'Thou art a God of seeing!' This implies that God has come to vindicate her right and protect her because he knows and has seen the wrong that has been done to her. It takes away her despair more than anything that could have been preached to her by Abram or Sarai.

Therefore she is now able to face the hard and humiliating act of obedience to which she knows herself now called by God: *Return to your mistress and submit to her* (v. 9). She can now go back with dignity and purpose, not because she has got to know herself better, but because she has got to know God better. Moreover, she is going back with something to say to Abram himself, something quite new to him, about the God he professes to belong to.

The collapse of conscience—and the cure

The worst feature of this whole incident is the collapse of conscience in both Abram and Sarai when the consequences of what they have done to themselves and their home throughout Hagar's pregnancy first becomes apparent. Neither shows any compunction, understanding love or tact. They fail even to attempt to control the sorry situation or to counteract its bitterness. It should have become clear to Abram that he had subjected Hagar to a use which should be suggested to no human being of any status, but he casually washes his hands of the affair and passes the responsibility to Sarai, even though he knows she is in an abnormally hard, angry and jealous mood—the more so because she knows she has been in error. *Behold your maid is in your power; do to her as you please* (v. 6). Sarai, who has led him on in the affair from the very beginning, simply blames him for all the woe and is sorry only for herself. *May the wrong done to me be on you!* (v. 5). And, having bitterly reproached her husband, she 'dealt harshly' with the girl, till she forced her out.

The return of the victim of their mad folly means the possibility of a return of conscience—especially when she comes back with the story of how God has seen it all, has stepped in to take her part and has sent her back as a witness! Now they can see who they are and what they have been doing. Under the guise of serving God they have brought to the verge of suicide one for whom he cares greatly. To further a scheme that turned out to be simply a self-conceived, self-centred piece of folly, they have played with the life and happiness of their maid and put at risk her whole future.

It is a remarkable fact that in this way God used the actual victim of their evil-doing to awaken their consciences and bring them back to some sanity. God has different ways of restoring conscience when it fails in different cases. To King David, when he had stifled every reproachful voice within him after his affair with Bathsheba, God sent Nathan the prophet with a word calculated to disturb and rouse him at the exact point of his cover-up and announcing clearly his guilt and punishment (2 Sam. 12.1). But with Abram and Sarai there is no such messenger on hand, and Hagar herself is used as their prophet. Their sin and guilt is brought back to them on her return, and they are allowed to see something of its enormity as they hear and see how it has worked itself out in their victim—and that in the very presence of God himself.

They could not otherwise come to understand the extent and scope and nature of what they have done. Hagar has preached eloquently to them without saying a word. Certainly she was not an innocent victim. She was well aware of the mischief she was causing to their plans and took pleasure in upsetting them. She, too, was foolish and played her hand recklessly. But in spite of her own measure of responsibility for the misery of her situation, it can be seen very clearly that she has been at the same time reacting, even though badly, as a victim of the wrong-doing of others. In this whole sorry affair it is she who has paid more than any of the others and borne the brunt of the suffering and shame that inevitably came as the affair developed.

We are therefore meant to look round and take stock of how things are working out for others because of us, and to question ourselves: Who within the circle of my influence today is the victim of my mistaken piety, my sheer lack of consideration for the feelings and hopes of others, my insistence on always having my own way in what I imagine is my own corner of the world's life? We can begin to ask, too, about the victims of the political policies, social ideals and national aims we support.

But if we are honestly on this track, we will ask ourselves about Jesus. Did he not come to make himself the weakest member of the family circle so that he could take all the worst that people could give upon himself? It is good for us if we can find our conscience becoming awakened—and cured—at this cross.

8

The Covenant—Demand and Promise

GENESIS 17.1–27

'You shall keep my covenant'

In Genesis 15 we read about how God entered into his covenant with Abram. As he did so he gave Abram a pledge that on his own side he would keep it for ever. It was God alone who, symbolized in the fire, performed the rite of passing between the pieces of the slaughtered animals laid on the ground. This rite was usually performed by both parties to a covenant, but then Abram was not involved by God. Now God wants Abram to allow himself to become more deeply involved in his side of the covenant and to listen carefully to what its obligations are. The purpose of what God does here is summed up in verse 9: *You shall keep my covenant.* Abram is to be told what this means.

No retirement

When he says, *Abram was ninety and nine years old* (v.1), the writer simply means that he was approaching what could then be expected to be retirement age! But God gave him a special pastoral visit, probably on the very day of celebration as he entered his hundredth year. And the message was that God expected more than ever before—and on a better standard than ever before.

The new creative powers released into this world through the coming of the blessing do their work independently, and sometimes in plain defiance of the natural strengths and virtues that normally prevail in our human battles and enterprises. Indeed, the more frail the human agent becomes from a natural point of view the more easily can happen the quite 'impossible' things that are so important in the furtherance of the kingdom of God.

The New Testament says the same thing: 'Though our outward man perish nevertheless the inward man is renewed day by day' (2 Cor. 4.16). It means that no Christian ever really 'retires'. No Christian has any right to imagine that his or her potential in the hands of God has somehow lessened now that a certain age has been reached. The answer of God to those who think they have reached the age and state when people normally pack up and retire is: 'My grace is sufficient for you, for my power is made perfect in weakness' (2 Cor. 12.9).

It is always especially sad that the Church in its practical work and pastoral concern seems sometimes to show a lack of understanding over this matter. Too often one hears laments from pastors that their congregations consist largely of the older generation. Perhaps this is how God desires to have it for the sake of a future full of promise, for there is often in the older generation a greater potential than in the younger for prayer and sacrifice—and we must note now that prayer and sacrifice are to become the most fruitful aspect of Abram's increasing usefulness in the service of God. We must therefore begin to see in our older generation the same potential as God saw in Abram, and challenge them to yield it. How bad a mistake it is for a church or a pastor to neglect the old in order the better to be able to wait on the young.

The whole covenant in one simple rule

In his greeting to Abram when he appears to tell him that his contract has been indefinitely renewed, God makes one great self-affirming claim and puts the essentials of everything he is going to demand of Abram in one simple rule of living: *I am God Almighty; walk before me, and be blameless* (v.1).

Abram is challenged specifically about the way he lives out his daily life. As we were reading through chapter 15 we saw him challenged about his basic attitude to God in heart and mind. The call to him there was 'Believe!' Here the call is 'Walk!' There God was concerned primarily about the justification of Abram before him (cf. p. 47 f.). Here he is concerned about the sanctification of Abram before him. Abram has to learn that his faith must be allowed to affect the whole way and direction in which he travels from day to day amid the hardships and temptations and opportunities on the everyday road of life. His faith has to govern even his walking style. It has to be allowed to affect the kind of step he takes as well as to determine the choice he makes between the byway and the highway, between the narrow or the broad, between the easy or the challenging. The word which Abram heard said to him was no less than that which the New Testament says so often to ourselves: 'As ye have received Christ Jesus as Lord, so walk in him' (Col. 2.6 AV).

The image of 'walking before God', as the Jewish commentator B. Jacob points out, implies freedom to choose the path. It is a different image from that used in the cases of Enoch and Noah, who are both said to have walked 'with' God (Gen. 5.22; 6.9). This latter image implies that God chooses the way and the man walks alongside. With the image used in the case of Abram the implication is that man is given full freedom to choose his way, though he is conscious of the presence of God and looks to God as he makes his free choice of the path he is to take. Perhaps the image comes from shepherding, in which the flock is directed by the calls of the shepherd, or from family life, in which the child walks before the eyes of the parent.

In making the choice of way and walk before God, our aim is to please the one who looks and sees and cares; feeling ourselves ever before the face of God brings both inspiration and restraint. 'Thou God seest me' certainly can become a subduing, correcting and even terrifying thought when our minds and hearts strongly incline us to evil. But we are meant to become more and more conscious of the presence of a God who is there to inspire rather than to scrutinize, for the quality of our mood and the strength and courage of our effort will depend greatly on the kind of God we imagine ourselves to be 'walking before'.

God therefore gives Abram a new name to think about as he receives this fresh challenge about his daily life: *I am El Shaddai* (v. 1 NEB). The strange name is translated in the RSV as 'God Almighty'. What it means exactly is disputed by scholars, who all admit the ultimate uncertainty of their conclusions. But we can regard it as a name that sums up everything that God had been to Abram up to this moment. He has already been called the 'Most High' God (*El Elyon* 4.19), and he has been given the strange title *El Roi*, which brought to the mind of Hagar comfort and hope when she felt forsaken (Gen. 15.13). Abram is already beginning to understand that he is a God for whom 'nothing is impossible' (Gen. 18.14). The Hagar episode has taught him too that God has his ways of intervening surprisingly in an emergency. But now it is made clear to him that he is to regard the whole of his life as lived in the presence of such a God. It reminds us of how unable we ourselves are to live the Christian life unless our minds are often directed to the almighty power of God to do for us the kind of thing he did for Jesus in raising him from the dead, and unless we listen to him, as Abram did, telling us who he is before he tells us what to do.

The final aspect of this demand on Abram is that he should respond with complete integrity—the same total integrity in his walk as he had shown in his self-offering attitude at the moment of his justification: *Walk before me and be blameless* (v. 1) is best explained by B. Jacob: 'If you want to become whole, which is my request for you, you must . . . place yourself under my exclusive supervision, guidance, and protection.' The phrase translated in our version as 'blameless' could also be translated as 'perfect'. What is implied is total surrender to God without reservation or rival motive. It means that there is never to occur any time when we 'let up' and let God down, no evasion when the demand is clear, no excuse for non-achievement.

The simple rule today

One simple rule! This is the first and only law of life that Abram was ever given. It could be applied as a simple pattern to think about when he was perplexed. It could become a simple test to let him know if he was going wrong. He is to be saved from the start from becoming lost in a complicated code of rules and regulations for his behaviour. Of course, as the social and political life of the people of God developed, problems became much too complicated for the simple rule and there had to be a more detailed spelling out of what it meant to walk before God in such integrity. By the time the covenant between God and Israel was renewed at Mount Sinai everything involved in Abram's simple rule for keeping the covenant was expanded and made clearer in the Ten Commandments (Exod. 20.1 ff.). And the work of later prophets and leaders was gradually to clarify and spell out what it meant for later generations to keep these commandments in a more sophisticated age. But even the prophets did not forget the simple rule: 'What does the Lord require of you but to do justice, and to love kindness, and to walk humbly with your God?' (Mic. 6.8).

Is such a simple rule helpful today? The problems of

living are much more complicated than ever before. Therefore we imagine we are beyond the imperative of any simple
rule. Many of us have been led to imagine that even the Ten
Commandments are much too simple to be relevant to the
kind of world we live in.

But the New Testament does not allow us to evade the
basic simplicity of the challenge that came to Abram. Jesus
himself lived the 'perfect' life and called men and women to
come after him with the simple command to 'follow'. Life is
not so complicated today that he does not go before us with
the same call, 'Follow me'. This lifts us above all the
complications and calls us to a decision that is all the more
urgent and comforting because we are brought back to such
a basic simplicity. And time and again in this teaching he
held his disciples to basic simplicities, echoing God's call to
Abram: 'Be perfect' (Matt. 5.48); 'Abide in me' (John 15.4);
'Hear my voice' (Rev. 3.20); 'Come' (Matt. 11.28); 'Ask . . .
seek . . . knock' (Luke 11.9); 'Believe' (Mark 9.23).

The whole covenant in one simple promise

What follows after this short and telling introduction of
Abram to his part in the covenant is a much longer speech of
God than anything so far given in the Bible. It goes into
details about the fulfilment of the covenant that we have not
yet heard about. Now it is made clear that the covenant
pledges *everlasting possession* of *all the land of Canaan* to
Abram's descendants (v. 8). The speech refers to kings who
will *come forth* from Abram's line (v. 6) and describes him as
the father of a multitude of nations (v. 4). It is made clear that
the fulfilment of the covenant is to come not through
Ishmael, but through a child born to Sarai herself, who is to
be called Isaac (vv. 15, 19), and it gives details about the
circumcision of all males as a sign of the covenant (v. 10 ff.).
Some scholars today do not like this chapter. They say that
it goes into too many details about the future to be a
convincing prophecy, that it lacks the dynamic, dramatic
and profound qualities of those sections of the story of
Abram that they attribute to other editors and writers. But

details matter to God as well as essentials. And though there are many new details here, the emphasis is not on them but on one or two very simple essentials.

As the promises are clarified to Abram, twice there is repeated to Abram a short promise summing up everything that is involved in the covenant on the side of God, in words as simple and as full of depth as any in the Old Testament: *I will . . . be God to you and to your descendants after you . . . I will be their God* (vv. 7–8). The promise 'I will be your God' sums up everything God is going to do to save, bless, judge and guide his people from generation to generation. Its meaning is to be gradually spelled out and clarified as time goes on. Indeed, all of the history written in the Old Testament is there to fill these words with meaning and to show us what it is for a people to have a God. And finally what they mean is shown to us in the birth, life, death and resurrection of Jesus.

When the covenant was renewed and discussed generations after Abram died, it was in these same terms that people were asked to grasp the full depth of its meaning. The whole section of the Book of Exodus from chapter 19 to 24 is the story of how God renewed the same covenant with the whole nation under Moses, and at the heart of this renewal are the words: 'I am the Lord your God' (Exod. 20.2) and 'You shall be my own possession' (Exod. 19.2). Jeremiah later looked forward to the day when the same covenant would be re-established in a new and better form, as a 'new covenant'. In that day, he affirmed, God would 'write his law' on the hearts of his people and 'remember their sin no more'. But even with all this, nothing would be added to what he had already promised, for the climax and essence even of this 'new covenant' is simply, 'and I will be their God, and they shall be my people' (Jer. 31.33).

The sign in the flesh

Every male among you shall be circumcised (v. 10). When he made the covenant in the first instance God gave Abram a sign of his pledge to keep it. A smoking kiln appeared and the tongue of flame leapt between the divided parts of the animal that had been laid out between him and Abram. Now God asks Abram to give his own pledge to the relationship. He has to become circumcised and has to circumcise every male born in his house.

Circumcision was an old rite, and it was at that time observed in many communities in the middle east. It was administered at puberty, for example, in Egypt as a sign of initiation into the priesthood. But in no community was it administered in infancy to all males. God therefore took this well-known rite, adapted it for his own purposes and attached to it a new meaning as he set it within the context of his relations with his people.

Even though it was performed in the first instance by a human agent, circumcision in Israel was always meant to be regarded as something done by God himself. The human agent was always to perform it in the name of the Lord as his operation in the flesh of his people. Calvin regards it as a kind of visible memorial of the covenant: 'As formerly covenants were not only committed to public records but were also engraven on brass, and sculptured in stones, in order that the memory of them might be fully recorded and more highly celebrated: so in the present instance God inscribes his covenant in the flesh of Abram.'

God meant circumcision to stand within the community life of Israel as a sign of his claim to the total, irreversible surrender of heart and life to himself—a sign of everything involved in the demand: 'Walk before me and be perfect.' Throughout the Old Testament, circumcision is always regarded as a sign that the inward 'heart' is given to God. People are appealed to circumcise their hearts (Deut. 10.16), and it is regarded as sheer hypocrisy to wear the sign of such surrender outwardly on the body and not to be entirely inclined to obey God from the heart. The hard-hearted man in the Bible is essentially an 'uncircumcised' person.

But it is emphasized also that in circumcision God lays claim to a man in his flesh. It is a sign that God wants from his people not simply a purely emotional and mental, or 'religious', response, but a response that involves the whole of the physical and social life lived out in the flesh. It is indeed an irreversible pledge to such a life of total obedience. A circumcised man can never become uncircumcised again and can never deny what has been done to him.

Circumcision is a sign that the whole community as one people, and at the same time each individual in particular, must come under the personal claim of God. Circumcision is emphatically a community rite. *Every male among you shall be circumcised* (v. 10), and *any uncircumcised male shall be cut off from his people* (v. 14). It is impossible to belong to the people of God without accepting this as the sign that encloses the people of God as one community. But it must also single out each individual personally and is to be regarded by each as a personal token of God's claim and possession of him as an individual. When God called for the renewal of the covenant at Mount Sinai this twofold aspect, communal and individual, of the claim and gift of circumcision is clearly brought out: 'If you obey my voice and keep my covenant, you shall be my own possession among all peoples: for all the earth is mine, and you shall be to me a kingdom of priests.' Each individually is called to be a priest, but this takes place only within the context of one kingdom and holy community (Exod. 19.5–6).

Therefore in circumcision God says to Israel, 'I want you each, I want you all, I want the whole of you all in heart, mind and flesh.' He does not say any less to us today, and nothing brings it out more clearly than our baptism, which is the New Testament counterpart of circumcision (cf. Col. 2.11–12). In it the one baptized is called by name, singled out, given himself the sign of being passed through the waters of death and resurrection (Rom. 6. 1–11), and yet it is a baptism and passage into a fellowship and unity with the whole Church and is given by the Church alone (1 Cor. 12.13). In it, too, we have the sign of a death, resurrection and regeneration that must be here and now an experience both of the inner life of those who are given it outwardly and of the total claim of God in Christ upon the whole of our life from the cradle to the grave, and in all its personal and social implications and outreach.

Miracles in the flesh

God has demanded of Abram the impossible: *Walk before me and be blameless—Circumcise heart and flesh—Give me your flesh to be the instrument of my service and the realm in which I manifest my kingdom.* But how foolish even such a demand! For in the Bible the 'flesh' is always recognized as that which is frail and naturally unyielding to God. When God lays claim on Abram in his 'flesh', he is demanding a response totally beyond the ability of any to give. And in Abram the 'flesh' is ninety-nine years old and perishing!

But in Abram himself there is to occur a miracle. He is to know and experience himself more fully than ever before as if he were a quite new man, and as a token of this new inner potential for life and change under God he is to have a new name, 'Abraham'. In the very giving of the name God pledges to Abraham the extra strength and assurance he needs to be able to bring his life in the flesh into obedience to God. The new covenant with God means life in a new order. Where there was no hope or possibility, there is to be hope. Where there was only 'flesh', there is to be spirit. Things that could not be under the old order are now to happen because people themselves like Abraham are to be made new under the Word of God.

And in Sarai there is to occur a double miracle. Her name too is to be changed as a sign of God's power to bring about the fulfilment of his Word through changing, turning and controlling the deepest inward springs of our human life. *Sarah shall be her name* (v. 15). *Moreover*, says God, *I will give you a son by her* (v. 16). He has the physical as well as the spiritual in his hands – and where he asks the impossible, he also (as Augustine suggests in his famous saying) gives the impossible. Exactly where he stakes his claim, he does his miracles. He began this day by saying to Abram in words, 'I am God almighty'. He finishes the day by promising to say it in deeds of wonderful grace and power.

The word, *You shall be the father of a multitude of nations* (v. 4), now spoken with complete assurance, must be taken to refer to Abraham not simply as the physical progenitor of a numerically increasing and healthy tribe of Semitic stock within the human species, but must be taken to refer primarily to Abraham's influence within the course of human history and culture and religion as a leader and example of total obedience to God and faith in his word. Men and women are to become his children as they hear the story of his belief, sacrifice and obedience, and as they are encountered from generation to generation with the same word as brought him out of Haran and made him and Sarah new creations before God. Jesus himself must have been referring in his mind to this particular promise when Zacchaeus responded to his teaching and love, and he pronounced him a 'son of Abraham' (Luke 19.9).

The response

Abraham fell on his face and laughed (v. 17). He simply had to. The presence of the gracious God himself was there before him, and the glory of the gracious Word humbled him with sheer gratitude that God should come and speak to such a one!

The laughter could be interpreted as an outburst of sheer incredulity, but it seems to accompany quite naturally Abraham's gesture of genuine reverence, and we can interpret it as the spontaneous outcome of astonished joy. The event he heard of, and believed, seemed so much beyond possibility that it could not be true, and yet it was announced with such firmness and authority that it had to be listened to. The combination of spontaneous reverence and completely free self-expression suggests precisely the combination of genuine awe and joyful confidence that we seek to attain today within all our best attempts at the renewal of worship. But we seldom come near to attaining it. When we seek to reproduce genuine reverence we become constrained and formal. We remain stiff when we fall on our faces, and we are unable genuinely to laugh at the same time. When we attempt to cure the dead formality by efforts to attain spontaneous joy and laughter, we lose all reverence. Abraham's response reminds us that utterly genuine awe can become one with pure charismatic joy when our worship is simply a genuine and spontaneous response to the astonishing promises that are clearly heard by us as they were by Abraham. Why should we have any more difficulty than Abraham in falling on our faces genuinely, and at the same time laughing genuinely as we open our ears together to God's astonishing promises, and our hearts and minds to the new life he comes to breathe into us—as we receive here and now from him the pledge and foretaste of the life of the world to come?

Yet, in the midst of the outburst of jubilant laughter and with astonishing boldness, Abraham lets it be known to God that he himself has been forming other ideas in his mind than those that had obviously been in God's mind. Time and again he has indulged in the hope that Ishmael is really meant to become the one through whom the promise will be transmitted to succeeding generations. He has learned to love and admire this child, who is after all his own son and there already. At that moment in the presence of God all these thoughts about Ishmael are clarified into either a verbally unexpressed wish or a spoken prayer: *Oh that Ishmael might live in thy sight!* (v. 18).

Of course the prayer seems to ask for a second best to replace the best. It seems to hanker after what comes by human effort rather than what comes by God's power alone. It indicates that Abraham is still prepared to argue a little against God's wisdom in dealing with the old affair with Hagar. It is a prayer that seems to want to drag God down to the level of Abraham's desires instead of to lift up Abraham's faith to God's level.

God replies, however, not with a rebuke, but with an affirmation that even this wish of Abraham, God's friend and partner in the new covenant, will be respected and will find its answer in its true place. *No*, he says. *As for Ishmael, I have heard you; behold, I will bless him and make him fruitful and multiply him exceedingly; he shall be the father of twelve princes, and I will make him a great nation. But I will establish my covenant with Isaac* (vv. 20–1). How encouraging it is for us to find that even the prayer to which God says 'No!' has not been in vain!

9

'Behold I Stand at the Door and Knock'

GENESIS 18.1–33

The appearance

The Lord appeared to him by the oaks of Mamre (v. 1). We have already heard quite frequently of such appearances, often at the altars, sometimes at other places. The close encounter between Abraham and God in the chapter previous to this one began with the Lord 'appearing' (Gen. 17.1), and at the end of the conversation we read: 'When he had finished talking with him, God went up from Abraham' (Gen. 17.22). We wish the writer had explained more fully what exactly was meant by the phrase 'God went up', for it seems to imply that while the Lord spoke to Abraham there was also something representing God visibly before his eyes—like that fire that Abraham himself had seen darting between the pieces of the divided carcase (Gen. 15.17) or that Moses saw in the bush (Exod. 3.1 ff.) or like the vision of a footstool of a throne with a distant, receding heavenly figure, such as Isaiah had (Isa. 6.1), or like the angelic figure that appeared to Joshua before his great battle (Josh. 5.13 ff.).

In this present instance, when *the Lord appeared* (v. 1), at first Abraham obviously does not know that this is the Lord! The Church Fathers and the Reformers when they read such things in Holy Scripture interpreted them as meaning that when God appeared to the Patriarchs like this he avoided showing them even a glimpse of himself as he is, but covered over his divine glory and presence with a disguise. Even though he was really there he hid the form of his glory, which would have blinded or annihilated those he was appearing to, and took on some other form of humiliation, thus presenting himself behind the appearance of such things as men, angels, fire, cloud and various visionary forms.

It is difficult to decide whether all three of the visitors present God himself to Abraham, or whether only the one in particular who often takes the lead does so. Some commentators hold that the story clearly distinguishes between the one who is always prominent in the conversation and the other two who are simply companion angels, but other commentators note how in the next chapter the two angels, or 'men', who go to Sodom after the leader has departed have full divine authority in their actions and judgements. Therefore all three are held to symbolize and present the Lord. Some commentators like the suggestion that here we have a symbol of the Holy Trinity.

God himself at the door

This 'appearance' meant the real presence of God there before Abraham. God himself was at the door. In the next chapter, when we read that on the same journey the two angels came to Sodom in the evening, it means that the Lord took the same divine presence there too. He did not merely flash an apparition before Abraham's eyes. The three men were not simply a symbol or representation of an absent God who all the while himself remained up in heaven. God is represented in these two chapters as actually taking a journey from heaven in order to be present in this real and special way both within the home of Abraham and in the night-life of Sodom. The service and hospitality in Abraham's home are given to the actual person of God himself. And what happens in Sodom before its judgement happens to God himself—not to a likeness or representative of God. This means that the presence of God before Abraham and in Sodom was a unique kind of presence, what is sometimes called a 'real presence'.

The Bible occasionally refers to God as being always

present everywhere, without our having to imagine him as coming to earth on a journey. Interpreting some of the teaching of the Bible about God, theologians sometimes speak of him as being both 'transcendent' and 'immanent'. For him to be 'transcendent' means that he always remains above everything that is and happens. He has his own place, his throne, his distance, his distinction from everything he has created, and is not immersed in anything. His being 'immanent' or omnipresent means that he is always present in everything, keeps everything in being and fills everything. The Bible does not deny either quality to God. Heaven and earth cannot contain him (Kings 8.27; Isa. 66.1; Acts 7.48–9), and at the same time he fills heaven and earth (Ps. 139.7–10; Jer. 23.23–4).

But besides all this the Bible occasionally tells us that though God is already everywhere in a general sense, there are times when he really comes to give places and people on earth special visits, and there are moments when people on earth thus visited by God are either specially blessed by such visits or specially condemned—the verdict depending on how he finds them. We can think of how God paid a special visit to the temple at Shiloh on that day when Samuel heard his name called from above the altar (1 Sam. 3.4). We can think of how he paid a special visit to David, when Nathan the prophet stood before him and preached a short sermon in which David heard not simply the voice of Nathan, but the voice of God present before him and speaking to him (2 Sam. 12.1 ff.).

In this particular incident now before us we are actually encouraged to think of God in his coming to Abraham as if he were actually on an unusually long journey. The whole story contained in chapters 18 and 19 is one story of a prolonged visit made by God to earth. He goes first to Abraham's home to bless it. Then he goes to Sodom to see for himself, close at hand, what it is like to be there. Of course in reading these stories in which God sometimes makes visits to earth, at other times even journeys on earth, and presents himself so invitingly and compellingly to people, we are very near some of the things which happened when Jesus ultimately came. For the gospel itself is the account of a very special and very prolonged visit—indeed of a sojourn of God on earth for a lifetime in a form not of glory but of utter humility—the 'Word became flesh and dwelt among us' (John 1.14). Jesus often spoke as if when he himself visited towns, market-places, homes and sick beds and met people, then the real presence of God was there when he was there. As they were given the opportunity of hearing him, of welcoming him, or of receiving his gifts and teaching, they were at the same time being given the opportunity of hearing and welcoming God himself. He bore himself and acted always as if his presence before such as Matthew, or Zacchaeus, or Pontius Pilate was the presence of the eternal God offering either grace or judgement. When he visited Jerusalem it was the time of its visitation by God himself (Luke 19.44).

This brings us back to the humble disguise God took in appreaing before Abraham and Sodom and helps us to think of another reason for it. God takes on such a humble disguise, because on this journey he desires to get in to the places where people live, and he wants to find the people just as they are when they are there. He already knows enough about the outside; how are things inside? But how can God hope to get in and really find out the truth unless he can take people, as it were, unawares? If they know too early who he is they will cover everything up too quickly and begin play-acting, and they will never be themselves in front of him. Therefore there must be nothing about the visitors to mark them off from the usual run of strangers on the road. If Abraham had known from the start who was visiting him, would he not have responded like the centurion who pleaded with Jesus to keep away from his home: 'Lord . . . I am not worthy to have you come under my roof' (Luke 7.6)?

The welcome

It may have happened with Abraham as it did with the two disciples who were met by Jesus on the road to Emmaus. At first 'their eyes were kept from recognizing him' (Luke 24.16), though they felt 'their hearts burn within' them (v. 32). But after they took him into their home to sit at table with them, 'their eyes were opened and they recognized him' (v. 31). We may suppose, then, that when Abraham *ran from the tent door* (v. 2) to meet his visitors at first, his haste was simply the unguarded spontaneity of one who was always keen to offer hospitality without question to strangers—though even at the beginning there may have been an unusual degree of inner excitement which he felt strange.

But soon Abraham knows with more certainty the importance of the visit and the visitors, and we find the excitement mounting. Four times in two sentences we find him running and making everyone else run: *And Abraham hastened into the tent to Sarah, and said, 'Make ready quickly three measures of fine meal, knead it and make cakes.' And Abraham ran to the herd, and took a calf, tender and good, and gave it to the servant who hastened to prepare it* (vv. 6–7). Undoubtedly at this stage the haste and excitement are caused by a sense of the infinite privilege he now knows to be his. How long can anyone on earth expect joy and glory to go on? Surely never again can the home and hospitality of a mortal man be honoured in a way like this!

From the start the excitement is mixed with a profound reverence. After the first burst of haste Abraham *bowed himself to the earth* (v. 2), and at the end, when the meal is fully prepared, he cannot bring himself to sit down. No one can be leisurely or casual in the divine presence. He himself must have the privilege of serving, for this does the greater honour to the guests. So he took all that had been prepared *and set it before them; and he stood by them* (v. 8).

Our mind turns to the visit of Jesus to the house of Simon the Pharisee. He reproached Simon:

'I entered your house, you gave me no water for my feet, but she has wet my feet with her tears and wiped them

75

with her hair. You gave me no kiss, but from the time I came in she has not ceased to kiss my feet. You did not anoint my head with oil, but she has anointed my feet with ointment (Luke 7.44–5).

'I entered your house'—but not a sign of joy or even honour, not a trace that anyone but this woman understood who he was, everything around him, except for her devotion, careless, casual and cold!

Abraham's excitement and reverence deepen as they continue. In our own religious experience it is too often different. The beginning is nearly always full of excitement—a deep interest in the Bible and Church, with reverence and wonder at each new discovery of what we have in Christ. But how often we revert back to the careless and the cold and the casual instead of making progress!

The three pointed questions

After the meal comes the business. God, as Abraham's friend, has come to consult him about what he is to do in one of the biggest social and international problems of his day: that of Sodom, its social injustices and its homosexuality. This is the climax of Abraham's day of astonishing privilege. He is being given a share of the responsibility of world government.

But there is a domestic issue to be settled before world affairs can be discussed. There is a sensitive spot in Abraham's family life that God first wants to touch with his finger so that it can be put right. Abraham has failed here in the home. This is brought out in a series of three questions (vv. 9–15) which God gently puts to him. Each is put in the context of the definite re-announcement of the great promise, now with a date attached. What a thrilling experience it should have been for the childless couple to hear it: *I will surely return to you in the spring, and Sarah your wife will have a son* (v. 10).

But is Sarah even to be allowed to hear it? *Where is Sarah your wife?* is the first very pointed, almost blunt question

(v. 9), quite like the blunt question which Jesus suddenly injected into his conversation with the woman at the well (John 4.16). It is a reproach to Abraham about what was going on there before God's eyes on this very visit. Abraham had neglected to bring Sarah in from her kitchen supervision for the after-dinner conversation. Luther blames Sarah herself: 'Sarah . . . like a tortoise remains in her little shell and does not take the time required to take a close look at the guests.' But we would be closer to the mark if we blamed the centuries-old male chauvinism that made it all the more difficult for God's word to come to the woman because of the role she was cast in. We surely must put the blame on Abraham, and surely this is the point in the very awkward question: that Sarah, instead of hearing directly face to face the word that concerned her so much, should merely overhear it when her ears were alerted at the kitchen door to a conversation that named her name. Immediately the significance of this visit began to dawn on him, surely Abraham should have whispered to her his thoughts about whom they had on the doorstep, and she should have been alongside him as he stood at the table she had helped so much to prepare.

The second question is even more reproachful and pointed. *Why did Sarah laugh?* (v. 13). The answer is obvious. She was completely taken by surprise—had never heard till then of such a thing and never thought even of the possibility. All she could be expected, even by God, to do was to chuckle to herself as she leaned on the kitchen doorpost—listening to those men!

The fact now becomes obvious that though Abraham had heard weeks before about what God was going to do in this house, the husband had not even tried to share it with his wife. It is significant that God does not reproach Sarah for her laughter. He reproaches Abraham. The pointed question is put to him and not to her, for he is solely responsible and to blame for the fault. She is so ill prepared for it, because he has failed to prepare her, and instead of what might have been a thrilling response of adoration and thanksgiving, there is an awkward moment or two of misunderstanding.

Abraham has to learn that he cannot begin to pass on his good news to the world and to succeeding generations until he has sought to share it more fully with his wife and in the home circle.

If the first two questions are directed specifically to Abraham, the third question is for both: *Is anything too hard for the Lord?* (v. 14). This too is a reproach. God takes it amiss when people do not assent to what he clearly promises because they do not see how it can come about. As he is honoured when people believe his word so he is dishonoured by unbelief. But it is also a direct word of encouragement to Sarah. She must lift her eyes off herself and realize that it is on God's love and trustworthiness and power alone that the fulfilment of his word depends. This word, and the thought behind it, were often prominent in the prayers of Abraham's successors. Jeremiah quoted it to God and God quoted it back again to Jeremiah when the latter was struggling to attain some hope in the future of his nation (Jer. 32.17, 27). It was repeated by the angel to Mary at the annunciation (Luke 1.37) and by Jesus to his disciples (Luke 18.27). The apostles were never weary of reaffirming it in a new translation: 'He is able' (Cor. 9.8; Eph. 3.20; etc.).

To Abraham the question is intended to come as a challenge. God has now revealed to him a sphere and aspect of his life in which he has not so fully as elsewhere sought to 'walk before God' and 'become perfect' (Gen. 17.1). Why is it that so many of us continue to fail exactly where the old patriarch did? We seem to be so strong alone, in private, before God. We are courageous and far-seeing in our social and international ethics. And yet we are so poor in our family relationships!

The consultation

And now God is ready to share his concern with Abraham over what at that particular moment were even more urgent affairs than Abraham's domestic problems and what in the eyes of the world of that day, at least, must have seemed more important. To make a better setting for the consultation about Sodom, God shifted the scene, taking Abraham out to the highway. *The men set out from there and they looked towards Sodom; and Abraham went with them to set them on their way* (v. 16).

The news is broken. Abraham should know that a great act of judgement around the area of Sodom may be about to take place—a disaster by fire almost as terrifying and memorable as the flood that had destroyed the world in the days of Noah. God has heard so many bitter cries of despair and complaint against the people and ways of Sodom that such an outcome seems inevitable. *Because the outcry against Sodom and Gomorrah is great and their sin is very grave, I will go down and see whether they have done altogether according to the outcry which has come to me; and if not, I will know.* (vv. 20–1).

God is consulting Abraham because he feels that he can trust Abraham to act as the interpreter of his mind and ways to others. What he is going to have to do may involve the complete destruction of the two cities, the immolation of the whole population of the area. God wants a reliable witness so that people can be taught to understand what is taking place as these things happen around them. He must ensure at least that Abraham is privy to his mind and will understand the event in its inner depth and meaning so that later generations can be taught from it about God's righteousness. As the NEB translates the passage: *The Lord thought to Himself, shall I conceal from Abraham what I intend to do? He will become a great and powerful nation, and all nations of the earth will pray to be blessed as he is blessed. I have taken care of him on purpose that he may charge his son and family after him to conform to the way of the Lord* (v. 17).

Abraham now becomes the first man in the life of the people of God to take the role of a prophet who can interpret God's mind to his contemporaries (cf. Amos 3.7, Prov. 25.14).

God also wants to consult Abraham because the situation with regard to Sodom, as far as God is concerned, is still open. He has not yet 'decreed' or 'determined' or 'pre-destined' anything. Anything can therefore happen under the ordinance of God. And so, beforehand, God wants to know what Abraham thinks about it all. Having tested him over the course of many years, he believes he can trust Abraham to help him finally to make up his mind about what it is best to do. In the government of the world he will not overlook the human wisdom and judgement that is coming to its maturity in this man. Abraham, moreover, has one of his best friends and companions involved in the fate of Sodom. Surely if there is a case to be heard for the place, he can state it. Now it is revealed to us more fully why God wanted on this journey to get into the inside of human life. He is listening all the time in order to hear from inside what people feel about the way of things on earth. And now he is asking Abraham to tell him. After all, one of the main ultimate purposes of the incarnation itself was that God might begin to know from within what are the sorrows and anxieties of the human race. What he is seeking to hear from Abraham is what he finally heard from Jesus himself.

The pleading

Abraham immediately proves himself sensitive about what is precisely the uppermost concern in God's own mind, and he puts it to him concisely and in unforgettable terms: *Shall not the judge of all the earth do right?* (v. 25). This must become God's chief anxiety—not to act in haste, not to involve too many in suffering because he has to punish others, not to have justified doubts cast on the rightness of his judgements. What about the innocent who may become the victims of a judgement visiting Sodom and the questions that may arise concerning his own justice? Is it possible for him to remain in the thoughts of mankind as a just and loving God when a whole community is blotted out by an obvious stroke of his hand?

Abraham warns God. Suppose there as many as fifty righteous in Sodom. How can the world bear to hear of a loving and just God who destroys so many righteous with the wicked (v. 23)? And now the prayer continues to pour out. Before God Abraham finds himself free to express his mind and opinions without reserve, free to pour out his heart and to argue—so much so that he becomes almost alarmed at his freeness: *Behold I have taken upon myself to speak to the Lord, I who am but dust and ashes* (v. 27). Yet he seems to feel that God wants him to speak, is listening intently and is ready to allow himself to be moved and his thoughts to be altered on the whole affair, as he and Abraham have this fellowship of concern about it. The situation is so flexible and what God is going to do is so undetermined that Abraham's mind and will on the matter can really change what is to take place.

Abraham is in anxious tension. His fellowship with God has helped him to feel more sympathetically with Sodom. He becomes an ardent advocate for those in Sodom who may become innocently involved in the possible disaster. 'The nearer Abraham approaches God, the more fully sensible does he become of the miserable and abject condition of men', says Calvin. He realizes that God has brought him into the affair in order to be their advocate and representative before him—and at the back of his mind there is the danger to his friend Lot. He feels that he is there to stand in for such people and to remind God from within humanity of what it is like to be in such a situation. It must be noted that the apparent conflict that now seems to arise between Abraham and God arises precisely out of the close fellowship over this affair.

Therefore Abraham boldly and persistently presses his views and his desires in the matter on God. The session of prayer even takes the form of a series of importunate requests in which Abraham seems to wring out of God a series of gradually reduced bargains on God's side about the conditions under which he is prepared to restrain himself from destroying the cities.

Unless we relegate this incident to a place in the album of curious Bible passages belonging to an age of primitive and unsophisticated piety which has long ceased to have any relevance for ourselves, it looks as if it has some quite startling things to say to us about what prayer can mean to us and to God. We must not tie our hands and tongues up beforehand with rigid theories and presuppositions that everything is predestined and that we are not able to change God's mind. God seemed to want to hear because he wanted to know. He seemed to be free and willing to make his decision in the light of what he heard. And it was as Abraham drew near to God that he discovered he could really talk boldly to him about things that beforehand he had thought should not be pressed too much by a creature before his Creator.

10
Sodom
GENESIS 19.1–14

The name of Sodom

The story of the destruction of Sodom by fire and brimstone was handed down so faithfully in Israel's tradition that the greatest prophets nearly always used it to illustrate their most dreadful and urgent oracles of warning and judgement. Jesus himself referred to it in his preaching.

Certainly the particular social sin that comes to mind today when the name of 'Sodom' is mentioned is that of giving full and free expression to unnatural lust between members of the same sex. We cannot deny that nearly all the references to such perversion in the Bible teach that it ultimately brings destruction to the health and stability of the society that encourages it. It is implied that it was precisely the growth of sexual perversion that brought about the ultimate downfall of the Canaanite communities before the possession of the land by Israel (Lev. 18. 24–5; cf. 20.13), and Paul felt that the same kind of punishment for the same kind of corruption was destroying Roman society in his own time (Rom. 1.22 ff.).

Yet it is remarkable that in the Old Testament accounts of what was really wrong with Sodom, the city is not blamed precisely for its homosexuality as such, but for the sheer cruelty that arose from the free and untrammelled expression of such a vice. Most of the biblical references to Sodom blame it explicitly for its cruelty to the weak members of the community, its entire lack of social conscience, especially its carelessness of the rights of the individual. It is stressed in the Genesis account of the situation that the 'outcry' from Sodom was unusually intense and passionate, and that it was the 'outrage' inflicted on its victims that forced God to take more intimate notice of it. Commentators point out that the Hebrew word translated by such terms 'implies, above all, arrogant disregard for elementary human rights, a cynical insensitivity to the sufferings of others' (Sarna). It is precisely this element in the sin of Sodom that is underlined by the prophets when they refer to the place. When Isaiah faced the pious yet cruel rulers of Jerusalem in his day, the best name he could find for them was 'Ye rulers of Sodom'. According to Ezekiel the sin of Sodom in its practice of 'abominable things' before the Lord gave rise to 'pride, surfeit of food, and prosperous ease' (Ezek. 16.49), leading to a refusal to aid the poor and needy. According to Jeremiah the sin of Sodom consisted of a whole community living in falsehood, so that 'the hand of the wicked was strengthened, and none turned from wickedness'. The implication is that where homosexuality is allowed to become the rule without restraint or warning, then a situation is bound to arise in which the strong and ruthless find their pleasure at the expense of the weak.

The story itself emphasizes the strength, universal compass and cruelty of the vice-ring that held the people of the city in its grip. No non-conformity was finally allowed in Sodom. Even Lot, whose home by sheer miracle had been unmolested till this final day of visitation, had in the end to choose to conform or be destroyed. For anyone to remain different was not tolerated. This was Sodom.

The public face of Sodom

Sodom gained such a name! Yet it could, in its day, put on a fair public face. It showed many daytime signs of strong law and order. The opening and shutting of the gates at dawn and at dusk showed that all the unruliness of the night and the works of darkness were shut out of this pleasant, safe place and that the conventions practised in daylight were those of a healthy community. On the surface everything looked stable and respectable. A strict moral code prevailed in many important areas of life. Strangers who arrived during the day were tempted to imagine that they could even spend the night in the streets of this place, behind the security of these strong, shut gates, without being molested.

So good did the public face of Sodom look, and so strong did their stabilizing conventions seem, that those who were in positions of responsibility were trapped into deceiving themselves. They were deluded into thinking that the culture of a city such as theirs had something to preserve and pass on to the world. They thought that non-conformity was irrational. They began to insist, indeed, that it was the former standards of decency that had been perverted. 'By custom,' says Calvin, 'they had imagined their crime to be lawful.'

Exposure before judgement

A central feature of the vivid picture of the great day of judgement in the twentieth chapter of Revelation is that 'the books were opened' and 'the dead were judged by what is written in the books, by what they had done' (Rev. 20.12). There all is described, all made clear and open so that all can know and understand the subsequent verdict. Paul underlines this aspect of the process of God's judgement when he speaks of the 'day when God . . . judges the secrets of men' (Rom. 2.16). How could justice under punishment exist unless it is clear that the punishment is justifiable?

But the exposure of Sodom is to be made not by calling witnesses, not by the accusing finger of a prosecuting counsel, but by the spontaneous and unguarded action of the people themselves. There suddenly arises in the city a situation in which all are thrown off their guard, and without pretence or restraint in one infinitely concentrated happening they themselves show what they really are. Everything was contrived to bring it about. The daylight ended. The atmosphere grew relaxed and the holiday mood was allowed to take over. The weather helped, it was a good evening and a beautiful night. The convention of Sodom was that under such conditions all convention ended and they really abandoned all restraint.

The story suggests that there was something in the potential victims that looked so good, beautiful and pure that it provoked the attack, for this thing is what evil most loves to drag down and destroy. Moreover, because they looked so weak and seemed such an easy prey, the worst elements in the life of Sodom were encouraged to throw off all fear and restraint and were given a new confidence to be at their very worst. So it all happened. For a moment, in the presence of the judge, Sodom became Sodom, and there was no need for a warrant, an arrest, the taking of evidence or any address to a jury—no need even for an entry in the books of any court. Jesus warned us that there would come times of exposure in the lives of all of us when 'the tree is known by its fruit' (Matt. 12.33). We may be able to conceal our badness or goodness for a while by conventional behaviour but ultimately we will be known for what we really are. He then went on to say that this revelation of what we really are will come out especially in our unguarded or careless moments: 'I tell you, on the day of judgement men will render account for every careless word they utter' (Matt. 12.36—AV has 'idle' and NEB has 'thoughtless' for 'careless'). Each of us, then, is only truly known, and we can only truly know ourselves, by what comes from us when we no longer put up a guard of conventional restraints against genuine free expression of the heart in these often quiet, perhaps often even unwitnessed moments of testing when what is inside is really allowed to come out.

This exposure is apt to happen especially when we are

faced by the stranger. We do not realize that the stranger who sometimes seems to wander into the area that we think is our specially private concern, or who happens to be laid there by the wayside as we pass through life, or of whose sorry plight we hear so clearly through our mass media, may be God himself challenging and testing us. He looks so ordinary, our encounter with him is so casual, the news we are brought about his plight is of such a common kind that we do not know that the decisions we come to about him are going to be written up in the book of our destiny. But this is what Jesus warned us might happen. When we are off our guard how often is he there before us, as he was on the streets of Sodom, as he was there before Pontius Pilate when he had to give his judgement, as he was there before those who denied him or abused him, as he was there that day when they took him and pierced him and crucified him.

The facts of the case

It was not only Sodom that was exposed on that night; homosexuality was also exposed. We are meant to notice the solidarity of the community in the vice. When they heard that two strangers had arrived, *the men of the city, the men of Sodom, both young and old, all the people to the last man surrounded the house: and they called to Lot, 'Where are the men who came to you tonight? Bring them out that we may know them'* (v. 4-5). They were all of one mind in doing what they did, all protest had been crushed for so long. We are meant also to notice the demonic nature of the spirit that seems to be the driving power in the community. They could not stop short of the perversion and destruction of the highest good, especially that which is chaste. They cannot bear to leave the beauty and sanctity of God's own image to shine unmolested in their midst. We are meant to be warned by the fact that Sodom and Gomorrah, marked by this particular sin, are singled out at this stage of God's redemptive and merciful work for such a severe and exemplary judgement.

It is made clear by this story, especially by its position at this stage in the Bible, that the great redemptive purposes of

God for mankind which are beginning to find their fulfilment in Abraham cannot possibly come to any fruition without the destruction of that which perverts the sex life of men and women. The purpose of God with Abraham aims at the redemption of this whole area of life.

In the light of the New Testament, a persuasive case can be made for the revision of some of our traditional attitudes to and sanctions against the individual who admits that he or she is as an exception in sex inclination and make-up, who seeks to live by the power of Christ's forgiveness and grace. None of us today, in the light of Christ's teaching, can too confidently condemn another where the individual expression and control of sex is concerned. But where the community is concerned, when lust of any kind is not deliberately put under by some kind of restraint, it can soon attain a demonic momentum that tends to crush things that are beautiful and tender. 'When the sense of shame is overcome, and the reins are given to lust, a vile and outrageous barbarism necessarily succeeds, and many kinds of sin are blended together' (Calvin).

The story seems to say that there is no justification for homosexuality and no nobility in it. It can lead to destruction and death. The self-affirming homosexual is self-affirming in that which God had to destroy, or it destroys that which God had made beautiful.

The final issue

The destruction of this city was the immediate result of a sordid attempt to violate two defenceless individuals who should have been given protection. They were 'outraged' and unprotected. There was no pity in Sodom. The heart-cries of individually outraged victims of its lusts and cruelty went unheeded.

When things are to be finally reckoned up in the last judgement it is precisely this kind of wrong that will be most severely redressed. When God looks at communities the first question he asks is about how individuals are feeling and faring, especially those who have no protector or belong to

defenceless minority groups. Are they being thought about
and listened to and cared for? God is the one who hears the
cries of the afflicted. He wants to know why and to go to
help them. 'I have seen the affliction of my people . . .
because of their task-masters . . . and I have come down to
deliver them' (Exod. 3.7 ff.). He looks into individual cases
and is angered when he finds a wrong: 'He looked for justice
but behold, bloodshed; for righteousness, but behold a cry'
(Isa. 5.7). Indeed every aspect of the plight of the wronged—
the pain, the shame, the loneliness, the loss—every bit of
damage done to the individual is measured in its breadth
and intensity by One who never goes astray in his assessment.

In the first part of Psalm 18 there is a description of God
upturning things everywhere on earth in his anger, scattering
his enemies with fire and thunder, rocking the whole earth,
laying bare its foundations, coming down to earth swiftly in
a chariot of storm and darkness, and the Psalmist affirms
that it all happened because he himself in a moment of
extremity called upon the Lord for his help and protection.
'He reached from on high, he took me, he drew me out of
many waters. He delivered me from my strong enemy'
(Ps.18.16–18). It is this intense concentration on the individual in his cry for protection and judgement that we find in
this strange story of Sodom.

Jesus warned us from this story not to be lulled to sleep
by the apparent stability of things around us: 'In the days of
Lot they ate, they drank, they bought, they sold, they
planted, they built' (Luke 17.28). But as in the days of
Noah, when they were eating and drinking and giving in
marriage and 'did not know until the flood came' (Matt.
24.38–9), so in Sodom they were completely unaware of the
corruptions of their customs and the hopeless instability of
their way of life. We too can become lulled to sleep by the
apparent strength of what has become established all around
us as acceptable and good social, political and moral customs.
'Watch', said Jesus, after he had reminded people about the
Sodom-like situations of the days of Noah (Matt. 24.42). To
'watch' is to become aware that the future lies with Jesus

and his kingdom and to examine all protests and cries of outrage in the light of this great and decisive fact.

11
Lot
GENESIS 19.15–38

The lingering strength of a good tradition

We are now given a last look at Lot. He had chosen to move towards Sodom many years ago, when the environment had offered good financial prospects to a man of his resources and skills and, as we have seen, had had its show of stability and decency. At first he pitched his tent in its outer ring (Gen. 13.12), and then he built or bought what seems to have been a substantial house near one of its centres of life. He must have been living there for some years while his daughters grew up and became betrothed. Till that dreadful last night he seems to have been the one man in the whole city whose family life had not yet been disrupted by the common vice. He still owed much to his own past family background.

The author of 2 Peter gives us his picture of Lot in Sodom: God 'rescued righteous Lot, greatly distressed by the licentiousness of the wicked (for by what that righteous man saw and heard as he lived among them, he was vexed in his righteous soul day after day with their lawless deeds)' (2 Pet. 2.7–8). He simply could not settle down happily in the place once he discovered what was there. Though he was obviously too much caught up in the trade and business life of the Sodom area to remove away totally, he obviously remained separate socially. He is by himself at the gate (Gen. 19.1) when we see him at the beginning of our chapter. He is alone facing the mob at night. He is reproached for thinking himself superior—'This fellow came to sojourn, and he would play the judge!' (Gen. 19.9). The fact that his family circle and his house had been left so long unmolested shows us how strictly he had kept his daughters apart from the crowd up till then. He cannot have thought out before-hand the implications of what he was saying, but even his shocking proposal to yield his two daughters to satisfy the lust of the mob, when the only other alternative was the violation of the two strangers to whom he had pledged his protection, at least shows the degree of his shock and horror over his discovery of the strength and extent of the vice around him.

The opening verses of the chapter also show us how much there was of Abraham still in Lot. He had the same open generosity for the stranger as had his uncle, the same concern to offer to the traveller protection from the surrounding dangers. It is at this point that Lot is shown in remarkable contrast to the people of Sodom, who saw in such visitors only a fresh incitement to their lusts. Indeed, the reason why Lot lingered around the gates of the city in the late afternoon was that he might forestall for their sake any possible danger.

So we seem to be able to produce at least some measure of virtue by education. 'Train up a child in the way he should go, and when he is old he will not depart from it' (Prov. 22.6). Even today a family tradition can become in later life the most powerful force for weal or woe. The law of God, if not written on the doorposts and gates (Deut. 6.9), can at least become written in the customs of the household.

The prayers of Abraham

Though the influence of a good tradition thus lingered on and deeply affected him, it was not this that saved Lot in the crisis, but rather the prayers of his uncle. When he is finally pressed by the urgency both of the angels' appeal and of the situation to make up his mind to get out of Sodom once for all instead of perishing within the city, it becomes obvious that he cannot make such a decision. Left to himself he will certainly be destroyed. Lot *lingered* (v. 16) even though he was being persistently 'urged' by the angels to make no delay, and it was by a purely gracious intervention of God that he was simply pushed out: *he lingered; so the men seized him and his two daughters by the hand, the Lord being merciful to him, and they brought him forth* (v. 16). It is at this point that we are meant to turn to verse 29: *God remembered Abraham, and sent Lot out.*

Prayers must go with education. We may provide for children the good home background, the educational opportunities, the religious and moral teaching, all in the context of a healthy psychological relationship with them, but unless at the same time, and long after our close contact with them is all over, we constantly, even unceasingly and always urgently pray to God for them as Abraham did for Lot—for his mercy and incredible power to be at work in and around them—we will fail them. Our continuing prayer alone can save them, especially in their moments of crucial moral decision, in the trials that can suddenly strain and snap their marital relationships in their temptations by the unbelief that seems today to overcome the strongest resistance when it is merely human.

Life has been so constituted by God that the prayers of others for us—even of those who have died—can always be a stronger factor in our lives than our own inner moral strength. This is why so many of us at times of temptation and decision can find ourselves seized by a love, a power and determination other than any that could ever have come from within ourselves, and we find ourselves enabled to let go, cut loose and move on in a new and better way. The basic saving fact in the life of all and each of us is that Christ himself ever lives to make intercessions for us (Heb. 7.25).

God sent Lot out *in the midst of the overthrow, when he overthrew the cities* (v. 29). It looks today as if God has decided again that much on this earth requires to be overthrown! This is why we have been passing through such rapid changes recently, and why so many international and social institutions and customs which we thought to be stable are now collapsing. The Epistle to the Hebrews speaks of God as sometimes 'shaking' the earth. But there are things

91

that can stand when everything else is being shaken (Heb. 12.26–27), and while God is busy with the work of demolition he has an ear for prayer and a willingness to save when he hears.

God remembered Abraham, and sent Lot out of the midst of the overthrow, yet when the answer to his prayers was being given Abraham himself looked such a futile and isolated figure. He *went early in the morning to the place where he had stood before the Lord; and he looked down toward Sodom . . . and lo, the smoke of the land went up like the smoke of a furnace* (v. 27). He stood on the very spot where he had been encouraged to pray boldly and had been inspired with confidence that God would hear. He had believed that God's will was to bless and save all nations through him and had hoped that the saving of Sodom might be a sign to him that God's Word was to be relied on. But now he is dashed and perplexed in his hopes and appalled at the thought of what might have happened, especially to Lot and his children. Of course in time he will hear the story and he will understand. He will come to know that in sending Lot out God has given him a sign other than the one he has looked for, that he is indeed remembered and that his praying is heard and answered. But like so many others in every age he thinks for a short time that his answered prayer has been all in vain.

Collapse in the moment of self-discovery

Now we have to watch the collapse of Lot. It is a remarkable feature of this story that its opening paragraph and first scene or two show us Lot as one who over a sustained period in Sodom bore himself nobly. His actions and attitudes shine out in remarkable contrast to those of all around him and his family circle. It is indeed because of this story that he is counted in the New Testament as among the 'righteous' (2 Pet. 2.7–8) and stands alongside Noah in the mind of our Lord as a noble example in a decadent society (cf. Luke 17.21–9).

But as the action proceeds the narrator draws for us a picture of Lot in bold, clear lines that break harshly into the rhythm of his previous picture, and he now uses colours that contrast completely with what we have so far seen. We must not seek to evade anything of what he now brings before us, because we have already seen a completely other side. The narrative is meant to be read as the story of an utterly absurd and tragic collapse which happened to this one man in a moment of self-discovery.

Till the fatal night Lot had still considered his own position in Sodom secure and influential. He had gone out early in the evening to meet these strangers, confident that he could offer them complete protection *under my roof* (vv. 2, 8). With genuine and neighbourly feeling he had called the men of Sodom *my brothers* (v. 7). He had believed that such an appeal would work and that the limits of common decency would be respected, for with many of these men around him he had been able to build up at least good business relationships—and had he not chosen sons-in-law from this group? Their words of contempt stung him most deeply: *This fellow came to sojourn, and he would play the judge!* (v. 9). He had interpreted their former marks of respect for him as meaning that he could take on the role of arbiter among them; and now he discovered that in their estimate he was nothing more than a paternalistic play-actor.

He was shattered to find that he had miscalculated everything around him. The shock brought complete personal collapse. The offer to betray his own daughters rather than the strangers (v. 8) can be read either as an expression of the confused rambling of his mind in the process of collapsing, or as a symptom of his already having lost every scrap of his moral integrity. Like the rich fool who thought he was secure, important and possibly also influential, because the world he had built around him looked so secure and his stake in it seemed great, he suddenly discovered that all his estimates of everything around him had been false, and he heard himself irrefutably called by his true name: 'You fool' (Luke 12.20).

Salvation as renewal

The word 'salvation' can mean simply being rescued, as from a shipwreck, or being pulled out of the rubble after an earthquake—like a 'brand plucked from the burning' (Zech. 3.2). In this sense it is equivalent to 'survival'. We survive as Lot eventually survived Sodom—spared, kept, sheltered by God.

But in the Bible the word 'salvation' much more often means being filled, blessed and indeed regenerated. Nowhere is this renewal aspect of salvation stressed more than in the book of Isaiah. There God, in delivering his people, is regarded as creating a new earth as well as a new heaven (Isa. 65.17) in such a way that everything around them is already different. Their journey through the desert from captivity into freedom is described as a 'going out with joy' and a being 'led forth in peace' (Isa. 55.12). For on the way along the very desert path they have to travel they find wells and rivers that already bring them the refreshment and the trees and shrubs that bring the joy and the fruits that belong to the new age (Isa. 35.6; 43.19–20; 41.18–19; 55.13). 'The mountains and the hills before you shall break forth into singing, and all the trees of the field shall clap their hands' (Isa. 55.12). And the people themselves are renewed on their very journey. 'Then the eyes of the blind shall be opened, and the ears of the deaf unstopped; then shall the lame man leap like a hart, and the tongue of the dumb sing for joy' (Isa. 35.5–6). They need not wait for it till the end of the road. Indeed, God begins to do it for them even before they start the journey: 'Behold I am doing a new thing; now it springs forth, do you not perceive it?' (Isa. 43.19). Even now the people of God are to have the 'oil of gladness instead of mourning, the mantle of praise instead of a faint spirit' (Isa. 61.3).

With Abraham, to be with God, to hear his word, to believe his promise and to serve him has constantly and unfailingly meant renewal. He is the man of the great future and of the new age living always victorious and always refreshed in the midst of everything around him that may be passing away, because he already perceives and lives by the 'new thing' that God is doing (Isa. 43.19). It is the tragedy and absurdity of Lot's choice that in deciding what kind of an exit he is going to make from the collapsing world of Sodom, he will not allow it to happen in this triumphant way. The survival mentality takes over.

The survival mentality

From the beginning, therefore, Lot is listless in his response. The command to flee comes to him from the angel. This in itself implies ample power to fulfil what is commanded. But when he is urged to hurry he lingers. Instead of grasping the opportunity to leave by his own effort and decision he has to be seized and dragged by sheer force (v. 16). It is to be survival rather than renewal.

And once outside the city he pleads to be spared the effort of going any farther than simply the minimum required to ensure the safety of his skin. God wants him to take refuge in an open and large place prepared for him up in the hills and completely away from the contamination and danger: *Do not look back and stop anywhere in the valley; flee to the hills, lest you be consumed'* (v. 17). But when Lot finally does reach even the fringe of the hill country it is only as a second choice and he is driven there only by fear (v. 30). The first choice of his heart is the little city in the valley, a tiny, closed-in place, and he hopes he may be left to stay there for ever. *Behold yonder city is near enough to flee to, and it is a little one. Let me escape there—is it not a little one?—and my life will be saved'* (v. 20).

It is a refusal to take what is offered. Being told what God wants to give him, Lot firmly says, 'Oh no!' (v. 18). We can detect a touch of sarcasm in the way the writer records the beautiful and pious formal prayer of thanksgiving which he uttered in the same breath with which he made his blunt and disobedient refusal. There is also a touch of sarcasm when he makes the choice of the little closed-in city—'such a little place!'—instead of the open spaces. Lot indeed is acting as if he belongs to the collapsing world around Sodom rather than to the glorious age of the new creation.

Was the writer not thinking of those among the people of God in his own age who like Lot were experts at uttering pious liturgical prayers but still continued to insist before God on a small salvation instead of a large one, on scaling down God's promises to well-defined dimensions attainable with little effort, and on a kingdom of God very much down in the valley and only a little distance from and very little different from the world they were used to living in?

The New Testament underlines the fact that salvation means transformation here and now by a quite astonishing renewal of heart and mind (Rom. 12.1) and that the kingdom of God into which we can enter here and now is like a royal banquet to which the guests can be unlimited because the supply for the feast is unlimited (Luke 14.16 ff., Matt. 22.12 ff.). 'I came,' said Jesus, 'that they may have life, and have it abundantly' (John 10.10). Paul reminds us in one place that if we are ever 'restricted' in our living of the Christian life the fault must be not in what God wants us to receive but in our own affections (1 Cor. 6.11).

The one is taken and the other left

Though Lot is so listless in his response to God's grace, once on the way he does not look back, for it has been expressly forbidden (v. 17). He is not defiant. Even for his disappointing half-way stop in the valley he pleads to God for permission before he dares relax (v. 18). But his wife pays no heed to the angel's warning and in an act of brazen defiance turns and looks. We are not told whether she is prompted by regret or curiosity. All we know is that she deliberately shows her disregard for God at the moment when everything depends on believing in him.

The difference between Abraham and Lot now pales into insignificance in the face of the gulf that here appears between Lot and his wife. 'Remember Lot's wife', Jesus said, and reminded the people of his day that when the greatest crisis of all comes in human life 'there will be two in one bed; one will be taken and the other left. There will be two women grinding together; one will be taken and the other left' (Luke 17.32–5.).

The issue

At the end of the chapter the writer again tells what happened with both scorn and pathos. We are meant to remember that in spite of the separation between Lot and Abraham after their visit to Egypt (13.1 ff.) Lot's own family tradition, as well as that of Abraham, was still in some measure oriented to the fulfilment of the promise. By this time the pathetic old man has been driven out towards the hills to which God has called him out of Sodom. He is driven not by any fresh zeal that has come to him to inherit more fully God's promises but simply by fear; he finally finds refuge in a cave-dwelling (v. 30) and in his brokenness takes to strong drink (cf. Prov. 31. 4–7). If we like to suspect that he had been for some time in the habit of indulging in strong drink at night, it may help us to understand why he was so stupefied in Sodom when the crowd came round his doorway. No doubt now in his drunkenness he indulges in reminiscences about his great days with Abraham and goes over and over again the story of the revelations that had come especially to his uncle and about how he himself was the only member of the family to go with him.

Somehow the tradition about the promise and the blessing to all mankind that is to come through their posterity has registered in the minds of Lot's two daughters. It is part of the irony of the story that the very hope of in some way helping to bring about the fulfilment of the promise encourages them to commit their final act of shame. The sooner the better, they feel: *Our father is old, and there is not a man on earth to come in to us after the manner of all the earth. Come, let us make our father drink wine, and we will lie with him, that we may preserve offspring through our father* (vv. 31–2; cf. v. 34). So they make him really drunk.

The daughters have by now lost all true respect for their father, so strict and severe at home—he had protected their virginity as they grew up—but in the crisis at the house door he had made them cheap (v. 8). We can almost excuse them for their cunning play on their father's nerves and weakness. Yet the story of their action is told here also with deep contempt. What they did had its issue in the birth of the fathers of two tribes, the children of Moab and the children of Ammon (vv. 37–8). But far from being a blessing, one of these tribes became a reproach to Israel and the other became a curse (Num. 25.1–2). This story of their origin was handed down in detail to warn the Children of Israel that there are ways of 'preserving offspring' through which God will bring no blessing. And yet, by the grace of God and as a sign that even Lot can still have his share in Abraham's posterity, Ruth, raised up in Moab, is brought back to Israel to play a decisive part in the fulfilment of the promise (Matt. 1.5).

12
Abraham and Abimelech
GENESIS 20.1–18

An approach to the passage

We now come to the story of an incident similar even in detail to what happened shortly after Abraham arrived in Canaan. He again becomes afraid to own Sarah as his wife in public. He believes again that her beauty will present a temptation to the pagan king nearby, who, he fears, will so desire to have her that he will not scruple to kill any rival husband to gain easy control over a defenceless widow. So again he passes word round that Sarah is his sister. Again the local king orders Sarah to be taken to his house. Again God intervenes before any step is taken to degrade Sarah. Again Abraham is rebuked and given gifts.

Many scholars find that the best explanation for such striking similarities lies in the suggestion that we have here two accounts of one incident—called 'doublets'. The one story, told and retold in oral tradition, was circulated here and there, took the kind of shape given to it in the circulation of folklore, and different variations of it arose in different areas. When the compiler of Genesis had to give final form to the collected traditions before him he had two distinct versions of this one, neither of which he cared to sacrifice, and he fitted one at one place and the other at another place in the story of Abraham. Many scholars carefully examining the text suggest that one of the versions belongs to the 'Yahwist' tradition, the other to the 'Eloist' but find that both refer to the same original incident. Luther had few difficulties with the passage. He explained that Sarah, even at ninety, was attractive because God had marvellously rejuvenated her. And he made the point that Moses deliberately records this incident towards the end of Abraham's life to prove that the saints are human and that God had continually to support them in their weakness in a marvellous manner.

It helps us in our interpretation of these stories if we do not allow ourselves to be offended by the similarities between them. We must, indeed, take careful note of the unique element in each story as compared with the other. Even a superficial reading of both will show us that the part played by Abraham differs, his motives are significantly different because his situation in each story is different. Abraham's behaviour in Gerar is to be understood exactly in the context of his immediately preceding experience in Sodom. His former behaviour in Egypt we have understood from quite a different context. In the present story, too, the attitude of the ruler is much more clearly brought out than was the case with the king of Egypt, and this feature also can be of great importance in our interpretation.

Abraham 'possessed'

We find an especially helpful clue to what has gone wrong with Abraham in the question put to him by the king of Gerar at the climax of the incident. This is well translated in the Jerusalem Bible as: 'What possessed you?' (v. 10).

Abimelech possibly knew Abraham by previous reputation and was unable to understand this recent phase of his behaviour. Therefore he puts it down to his having allowed himself to be controlled by something alien to his normal, healthy outlook and disposition.

Abraham seems to have given way to one of those moods of depression and gloom that we find on certain occasions temporarily taking possession of the lives of many of the great men of God in the Bible, colouring their outlook, spoiling their vision and preventing them from behaving rationally and sensibly before God. It happened frequently to Jeremiah at one stage in his life (Jer. 12.1 ff.; 20.1 ff.). It happened to Elijah (1 Kings 19.4 ff.) and David (1 Sam. 27.1 ff.) and of course to Thomas (John 20.25). A gloom came over them which they allowed to settle down, to cling and to stick to the soul and mind. Their work was, for a short time, spoiled; their success was checked.

It was the effect of the Sodom affair that brought this gloom over Abraham. Just before this chapter begins we are given a glimpse of him as he 'went out' early in the morning (Gen. 19.27) and stood on the very place where he had poured himself out in intercession to God for Sodom. There he had received a promise that seemed to make its salvation certain: 'For the sake of ten, I will not destroy it' (Gen. 18.32). But there it was: not a house of it spared. 'And lo the smoke of the land went up like the smoke of a furnace' (Gen. 19.28). He knew what it meant: there had not been there even one family beside Lot's to earn one more chance to repent.

Soon after, he was bound to hear the inside story. Lot's daughters, too, must have talked and tried to explain their pregnancies and their father's state of mind. And Abraham, understanding more deeply than any other man on earth just what must have taken place in the streets of Sodom and just how far even Lot himself, the one righteous man, had sunk, allowed for a moment a mood of depression and fear to take possession of him.

Twice Jesus said to the disciples in the upper room when he was leaving them, 'Let not your hearts be troubled' (John

14.1, 27). And after the resurrection, when he came to Thomas, who had allowed himself to become intensely full of gloom, Jesus challenged him to stretch out his hand to touch his risen body, saying, 'Do not be faithless, but believing' (John 20.27). In each of these sayings he is commanding those around him not to allow their minds and hearts to be possessed by such moods.

The blinded wanderer

Abraham had become unsettled as well as depressed. Again instead of being led by the word of God he was driven this time by his own tormented heart. He wanted to get as far away as possible from where Sodom could even be seen. He journeyed towards the territory of the Negeb and dwelt between Kadesh and Shur, and he sojourned in Gerar.

It was providential that God had taken him to one of the few places in the whole land where, if he would only look around him, he would find cause for thankfulness instead of depression. Here everything was in contrast to Sodom. In Sodom, if the people had any religion at all, it had not the least reforming or healing effect on their ways and customs; in Gerar their daily life was lived under a *fear of God* (v. 11) that affected their whole outlook and life-style. In Sodom community solidarity found its expression in the common pursuit of vice; in Gerar a pious, upright king gave a lead, and all his servants followed him in a genuine act of community repentance (vv. 14 ff.). In Sodom the wronged and violated individual had no redress in outrage except to cry to heaven; in Gerar even the suspicion that one innocent person might have been wronged brought a public inquiry and a restoration of rights (v. 16). In Sodom the visiting divine strangers were singled out to be raped; in Gerar the wandering prophet of God from another nation was recognized, given his status and gifts and honoured.

Abraham therefore has now been brought into the midst of a community enjoying a large measure of the grace of God, healthy enough and stable enough under such grace to offer Abraham the protection he and his family need. If he had looked around him at what he had been led into, his life would have been cheered by the signs he could have found of the simple goodness and sweetness that ordinary human life itself can have where the grace of God is allowed to prevail. But all that happens to Abraham when he arrives in Gerar is that he wraps himself up tighter in his gloom and fear and thus allows himself to become completely blinded to the goodness around him. He does not look. He insists on remaining cut off within himself, and the old haunting suspicion of his earlier years, which brought him into such shame in Egypt, again returns: *They will kill me because of my wife* (v. 11). And so, as Lot errs tragically one way—by naïvely allowing himself to imagine there was some good even in Sodom when there was none—Abraham errs in the opposite way by naïvely imagining that there was no good in Gerar when it had so much to offer him.

The life, work and words of Jesus show us that evil is strong, pervasive, subtle and desperately destructive. We cannot get beyond the need to watch and pray (Mark 14.38) and put on the whole armour of God (Eph. 6.11). There are centres of virulent evil in the world around us today and we have to be aware of them. But Christ has already destroyed not only the chief works of the devil but also the power of evil to enjoy undisturbed rule anywhere on earth (John 12.31). While we cannot cease to watch, we must be prepared to look for signs around us and to listen to words around us that might already bear witness in perhaps unexpected places that Christ has been at work here and there in the surrounding environment, relieving us from the necessity always to live in hopeless tension with and suspicion of the world around us.

The healing of Abraham

God does not cure Abraham's depression this time by any kind of direct communication or vision (cf. Gen. 15). He speaks to the king of Gerar in a dream, restrains him from doing anything rash or harmful to the strange wanderer and teaches him something of his coming kingdom and about his promises to the world through Abraham. Abimelech is told that Abraham is a prophet who will pray for him and through whom he is meant to receive blessing (v. 7). He is warned that this stranger is a man whose presence and welfare are so important to God that anyone who does him real harm will be destroyed. God fills the heart of Abimelech with deep anxiety for the honour and welfare of Sarah—as if he understands something of the significance of her pregnancy.

What does Abraham begin to think of himself when all this is conveyed to him? This man Abimelech is taking the promise about his future and his seed and about Sarah more seriously than he himself has done. He is calling him back to his faith! From Abimelech he now has to receive pardon if things are to be put right, and through Abimelech he is brought to realize how urgently he needs to seek the pardon of God. His healing has begun, and the turning-point is the ministry of the king of Gerar.

Our Lord did not require such healing or forgiveness as did Abraham. But he did require encouragement, and the Gospels show him receiving it not only directly from heaven (Luke 3.22) but also from the ministry of humble and strange outsiders. There was racism in Judaea and the despised were the Samaritans, the kind of people from whom one could expect the worst. But when ten lepers were cleansed, only one had faith and only one returned to give praise to God at his feet, and he was a Samaritan (Luke 17.17)! Jesus' heart was thrilled. And there was the woman of the same race at the well who in her response to him gave him in his hunger 'food to eat', the effect of which completely astonished the disciples (John 4.32). Also there were the Greeks whose approach to him seemed to elate him on his way to the cross (John 12.23), and there was the dying thief (Luke 23.42). They all seemed to be beyond the pale, but he was wise enough and humble enough to take what they had to give him, for it too came to him from God.

Note Abimelech's deep concern for Abraham's welfare. As he listens to Abraham's story (vv. 11–13) something moves him to have compassion on the man who has stripped

103

himself of so much to become a wanderer on the face of the earth for God. He not only showers gifts on Abraham himself, but tries to ensure the vindication of Sarah (vv. 14–16). And he freely offers Abraham protection, hospitality and privilege within his kingdom. *Behold, my land is before you; dwell where it pleases you* (v. 15). Luther makes the comment: 'This king belongs to the catalogue of the saintly rulers whose duty it is to support the prophets and defend the Church of God, not to build monasteries.' At least the incident reminds us that if God inspires outsiders and even governments to generosity towards the Church we need not quench the Spirit by being too proud to accept thankfully the gifts and privileges given to us for his service, as long as we remain free to journey on as God wills.

The healing of Abimelech

Not only is Abraham healed by Abimelech but Abimelech is also healed by Abraham. In the word of God that comes through Abimelech to him he is reminded that it is his duty to pray for the welfare and healing of Gerar (v. 7). He requires the reminder at this time, for he is beginning to fail to pray for the world to which he is destined to bring blessing. How can he bring blessing except by prayer? He had prayed fervently enough for Sodom, but he has begun to tire. He must come again to realize that this is one of the main reasons why God is looking after him so carefully and blessing him so much—that he should pray. And he is to be shown that by his prayers he can meet the deepest and most urgent needs of those around him. *Then Abraham prayed to God; and God healed Abimelech, and also healed his wife and female slaves . . . For the Lord had closed all the wombs of the house of Abimelech because of Sarah, Abraham's wife* (vv. 17–18).

There was little else that Abraham could do for Abimelech, except to pray for him. In the way of achieving many of the great goals that make for a cultured and stable society Abraham had nothing else to give him and nothing to say to him. Abimelech could make wealth and war and peace. He could do many things for himself better than Abraham could do for himself. But he could not pray, and Abraham was placed there by god to do it for him. Otherwise all his great efforts at building a healthy nation and society would have failed.

'Unless the Lord builds the house, those who build it labour in vain. Unless the Lord watches over the city, the watchman stays awake in vain' (Ps. 127.1). With all our statesmanlike vision, our self-denying effort, our moral and political vigilance, we can achieve something impressive in the way of a city, but it cannot have ultimate stability and fruitfulness unless there is the constant healing and guidance that are given to a community because God inspires and answers prayers. 'Behold,' they said to Elisha, 'the situation of this city is pleasant . . . but the water is bad, and the land is unfruitful' (2 Kings 2.19). Without the ministry and blessing and prayer of the prophet, the streams that gave the place life were unhealthy and produced barrenness!

So we have to pray 'for kings and all in high positions' (1 Tim. 2.2). The Church is placed by God in society for this to have priority among all its ministries to a world that has so much that it needs little else. Samuel had to admit it, even reluctantly, when he was forced to resign his task of governing Israel and hand over to Saul: 'Far be it from me that I should sin against the Lord by ceasing to pray for you' (1 Sam. 12.23). Exactly here we Christians must rediscover what our main part is in human politics.

The grace of God in Gerar

We are unable to explain Gerar except by affirming that the grace of God was active within the whole community life. Theologians have sometimes called what happened in Gerar a result of the 'common grace' of God. The implication is that even apart from the acceptance of the Christian faith God desires and provides for the preservation within human life of a basic stability, moral goodness and a healthy measure of culture. It was the acceptance of their 'common grace' that made Gerar Gerar. But God means this grace to be enjoyed everywhere 'he makes his sun rise on the evil and the good, and sends rain on the just and on the unjust' (Matt. 5.45). It is God's will that even where the Gospel has not been heard or responded to, people should be able to share in this common form of his goodness and should have access to the ordinary happinesses of life in this world.

Having read about Gerar, we can now understand Sodom. What we have called the 'common grace of God' must have been rejected by Sodom as a community. They had rejected nature itself before they finally rejected the messengers of God. Sodom became Sodom only because it somehow, deliberately and absurdly, rejected the grace of God that would have kept it a healthy and prosperous city like Gerar.

13
The Birth of Isaac
GENESIS 21.1–13

After the earthquake—the pregnancy

Two cities have been contrasted, now two types of visitation. What happened when *the Lord visited Sarah* (v. 1) is brought into sharp contrast with what took place when he also visited Sodom. Then, as we have seen, there was thunder and earthquake, fire and brimstone. Now there is a quiet and hidden miracle—a pregnancy! Both are works of the same God who went from Abraham's home to the gates of Sodom. He did not change his nature on the course of the journey. He did not put on an act alien to himself when he was so cruelly received by Sodom. We must not think of him as at one time in a mood of gentleness and love, giving himself to one type of work to be singled out from the rest of his actions as a particularly saving work, and at another in a mood of anger and zeal for judgement, giving himself to another purely negative kind of work. On the contrary, both works are consistent expressions of what he always is. We are to think of him as no less himself, no less loving in the moment when he calls for the fire to fall on Sodom, than in the moment in which he revives Sarah and ensures that she shall have her son. He is as gracious in his acts of judgement as he is just in his acts of mercy.

The greater the work the quieter the way

Yet we are undoubtedly meant to evaluate the miracle of pregnancy as a greater work than the miracle of the earthquake fire that destroyed Sodom. Of course the latter kind of work makes a much quicker impression on those who crave spectacular and dramatic signs, on those who want hot news to sell to a world that craves sensation more than truth. What a scoop for any reporter to be the first in on that disaster. Puny little Isaac whimpering there in his cradle certainly arouses some curiosity as the progeny of two ninety-year-olds! But then, as now, everyone knew that the strange biological processes that throw up such a bewilderingly varied stream of new life into this already fascinating world can naturally produce all kinds of anomalies.

The New Testament especially reminds us that throughout the course of earth's history, however great may be the achievements that crown great empires or the disasters that destroy them, and however awesome and sensational may be the convulsions of the natural world through volcano, storm or earthquake, it is not chiefly through such spectacular processes that God is going to bring about advances in his kingdom.

'The Kingdom of God', said Jesus, 'is as if a man should scatter seed upon the ground' (Mark 4.26). He likened the way the kingdom of God comes on earth to the way seed is sown, received on the ground and germinated in the soil (Matt. 13.1–9). 'The sower sows the word' (Mark 4.14). What brings about the Kingdom of God in this world is what happens as one mind and heart communicates with others through quiet and deliberate speech and gentle acts of love and compassion. It is such speech and acts bearing witness to the kingdom that allow its light and life to penetrate other minds and hearts to bring about renewal and radically to change thoughts and feelings and values. Thus one living being quietly but eternally influences or is being influenced by another. Thus powerful and utterly revolutionary ideas are sown in minds, germinate and spread under the surface of things, creating deep new springs of spiritual life which ultimately cannot fail to make their mark slowly but surely on human history—even to alter its direction. And thus, too, souls are brought to new birth as surely and quietly as Isaac was brought to birth in the womb of Sarah.

'The Kingdom of God', said Jesus, 'is not coming with signs to be observed; nor will they say, "Lo here it is" or "There" ' (Luke 17.20–1)—or, as Cruden puts it in his Concordance: 'That Kingdom which God will set up in the world, will not become conspicuous and remarkable by any outward splendour or worldly pomp, but by its inward power and efficacy upon the hearts and minds of men.' Certainly events like the judgement that fell on Sodom may have to take place now and then, here and there, as obstacles to the spread of the kingdom have to be removed, but the real advance comes 'not with observation' (Luke 17.20 AV).

Let us not, then, become too concerned when the Church does not hit the headlines and when its programmes fail in spectacular revolutionary effect. Nor let us be too jubilant when we think we have achieved something that registers well in the statistical realm and even brings in the newsmen to give us momentary mention in a central page. And let us ask ourselves whether we really are nurturing within and around our congregations the quiet, life-giving processes which, often in simple, sincere conversation, impregnate the human mind with thoughts about, and thoughts from, a God who dwells 'in the high and holy place, and also with him who is of a contrite and humble spirit' (Isa. 57.15), whose most powerful way of working is clearly reflected in the earthly work of his dear son and whose crowning act of omnipotence and glory was in his death on the cross and his resurrection two days later.

After the waiting—the proof

Up till now, if Abraham and Sarah had been asked to produce something to prove that God's word actually did come to pass, they would have had great difficulty. They had no evidence at all when they left Haran that God's word was true—only faith. When they arrived in Canaan they were given no proof that the destiny of the people of God was to be worked out in this land—only a word which called for faith. Strangely enough, and as if by an inward miracle, without any external proof they believed.

But now, quite late in life, long after faith has begun on Sarah's part and after a long career based on faith on Abraham's part, both together are now given the evidence of sight. There is the child in Sarah's womb. It had been an impossibility but God had actually spoken to them before it had happened. And what otherwise would have been a freakish biological happening becomes for them a miracle witnessing the truth of God's word (cf. Heb. 11.11).

It can happen to us as it happened to them. Faith begins with the word. In the circumstances around us there may be nothing but what simply contradicts faith. But the word comes to us as it came to Abraham and Sarah—and faith comes to us. It comes as the opening of the eyes to see, beyond all possibility of proof, what the word affirms, and with the offering of the heart to believe, beyond all possibility of proof. Start with a 'faith' that rests on the evidence of miracle and you will go on craving to live by such evidence and your faith will never grow. Try to read yourself into the faith and you will soon, as easily, read yourself out of it. Try to convince people by confirmed historical evidence that Christ rose from the dead and the kind of Christian faith they will come into will tend to depend all along the line on such proofs and will be ineffective and unstable. If our faith is to be really healthy, then instead of beginning with proofs and signs and miracles it may begin even with laughter—the kind of incredulous laughter we have already heard from Abraham and Sarah (cf. 17.17; 18.12). Indeed, those who first laugh at the impossibility of what faith is expected to believe often become the best kind of Christians.

But to those who wait—in faith—proofs that their waiting is not in vain are sometimes given. Again it can happen to us as it happened to Abraham and Sarah. Proofs are apt to mount up: the fulfilment of so many of the hopes that were raised in our minds and hearts from the start by the promises of God, the answers to many of our persistent prayers. We believed once without seeing. Now we see. And our faith is the stronger for this kind of confirmation.

God-made laughter

We are meant to note the relaxed and astonished pleasure which the confirmation of her faith in God brought to Sarah at this stage in her life. She is pictured here chuckling to herself over her own feelings. Previously she had laughed in unbelief when she had first had to face the possibility of it (Gen. 18.12). But this laughter is quite different. It is God-made laughter—the laughter of sheer delight! *God has made laughter for me . . . Who would have said to Abraham that Sarah would suckle children?* (v. 6). It is like the laughter of the Psalmist when he too saw the word of God turned into a contemporary miracle: 'We were like those who dream. Then our mouth was filled with laughter, and our tongue with shouts of joy' (Ps. 126.1 f.). It is quite private laughter too. She is aware that other people will laugh when they hear of it: *Everyone who hears will laugh over me* (v. 6). But theirs will be a quite different kind of laughter than Sarah is enjoying to herself. It will be the laughter of the cynic or the unbeliever; 'They will condemn me as a lustful old woman!' is Luther's interpretation of this part of the text.

Though our own Christian life must be always basically a life of faith, we should at least credit God with being willing and able still to give us the delight of such God-made private laughter over the extraordinary things that at times he does to us. These may take the form of incidents and events we would not dream even of discussing with other people—who might laugh in a quite different way. But between us and God there is a private chuckle! Far too many of us shun even the idea of taking much notice of such signs, far less of seeking them. But in the life of faith we need not expect always and only to find ourselves engaged in a grim struggle to believe. One of the Psalmists who was obviously very sober in what he expected from God prayed to him: 'Shew me a sign of thy favour' (Ps. 68.17). Such signs, occasionally given and occasionally accepted by us, might help us to live more cheerfully and fruitfully in the service of God.

The word comes to the woman

And now, suddenly, we find that Sarah is not only pregnant with Isaac, but also pregnant with truth. Though she has obviously always been a woman of strong character, up till now her part has been mostly to follow her husband, to try to share his faith and his lot and to give in to him. On the one occasion on which we have seen her giving him advice she bungled very badly. But now something new has taken place. By herself and alone she has been given a new and important insight to follow through which is going to have momentous consequences in the life of the people of God. She feels that she herself has heard a word of God meant not only for herself but also for Abraham. She demands to be heard and obeyed; and her husband, against his own judgement, has to give in.

It would be very easy for us, reading the narrative superficially, to come to a very unfavourable judgement on how and why Sarah came to her important decision. We could regard her as a very interesting psychological case-study and draw close parallels between what we think happened to her and the kind of thing we see happening around us sometimes today. We can see it all: young Ishmael is now feeling grown up. He has been very much the family pet. Now he feels displaced, and he wonders why so much fuss is being made of the old woman's puny brat and the birth about which he has heard coarse jokes. We can imagine him teasing, taunting and perhaps insulting the youngster.

We can also imagine what might be in Sarah's mind at this juncture. Of course she is angry at what she has heard from the mouth of this *son of Hagar the Egyptian* (v. 9). There is a certain amount of racism and a good deal of class distinction in her mental reference at this stage. Moreover, Ishmael reminds her acutely of her past stupidity. The coming of Isaac has proved that Abraham's previous child was the mistake of her life. In venting her rage on him, she is venting it on herself and her own past. So it all comes out: *Cast out this slave woman with her son; for the son of this slave woman shall not be heir with my son Isaac* (v. 10).

In this way we could let our minds work on the problem and judge Sarah 'after the flesh' (cf. 2 Cor. 5.16 AV). But God approved of Sarah's decision and gave it his blessing. This does not mean that we have to whitewash her. Again we must avoid the line that Luther takes in making her a 'heartbroken' martyr who in calling for the expulsion of the other child 'killed her own innate feelings'. Our motives are never pure even in our best service of God. But on that day of the celebration of Isaac's weaning, Sarah's decision and her deed both arose from the insight and working of faith in a moment of truth. 'I do not doubt', says Calvin, who clearly saw the other side of the affair too, 'both that her tongue and mind were governed by the secret impulse of the Spirit, and that the whole affair was directed by the providence of God.' Paul, when he wrote Galatians, thought deeply about this incident and held up her action here as a shining example (Gal. 4.21 ff.).

The truth comes to her in a flash as she watches the two boys playing; she suddenly sees them as the products of two completely incompatible outlooks and ways of going about life and of trying to do service to God. Isaac, beyond all doubt now, is the product of their waiting on God, of the word of God and the way of faith. But now, suddenly, Ishmael rises before her mind as the product of an entirely other way—of the way she herself and her husband took— the way of human wisdom, the way of confidence not in the word of God but in what the New Testament calls the 'flesh', meaning by this term everything centred on the independent, self-determining human will. She now cannot help seeing that one boy belongs to a world of ideas and ideals that can never mix with the world of ideas and ideals to which the other belongs. She cannot help seeing in the conflict between these two boys completely opposite attitudes and outlooks. Ishmael therefore now stands in her eyes for everything that threatens the healthy and full development of the good that lies there in the child Isaac, who is the product of the grace and word of God. There can be no toleration of the one by the other, no freedom for the one except far away from the other.

She has therefore no hesitation in sharing with her husband, as the word and command of God, the great conviction that has come to her: *Cast out this slave-woman and her son* (v. 10). She is pleading with him to see it as she has seen it, to open his eyes to these simple but infinitely important spiritual facts of the case and to make a clear decision there and then about the whole Hagar affair, about his own past, and to acknowledge his dreadful mistake in having so tragically reverted to a way and an outlook that could never become the way and outlook of the people and the kingdom of God.

The submission of Abraham

In this chapter Sarah thus finds for the first time her responsible place of leadership in the family of God. This is the first time in the Bible in which the will of God is reached after a discussion which obviously must have taken place between man and woman. In this case, under God, the wisdom, advice and will of the woman prevails over that of the man and thus God's will is found. Moreover, this happened not over a trivial, merely domestic matter, but over a matter of utmost importance for the shaping of the whole future life and outlook of the people of God. Indeed the ultimate separation between Arab and Jew was involved in this decision to separate Isaac from Ishmael—and the political consequences of such a step are evident today.

It happened in a matter that touched Abraham himself in a much more intensely personal way than it did Sarah, for the boy Ishmael was his son and not hers. He himself had prayed long for this child, that he might inherit the promises (17.18). Perhaps it was this very fact that made it all the more necessary for the word of God to come to Abraham through Sarah. Abraham could never have come to the point of making such a decision by himself, and his mind was set against it in a way that was deeply antagonistic. Possibly, too, his natural bent of mind was different from Sarah's and he himself could not have seen the issue as a whole so quickly as she intuitively did. At any rate, he is finally forced by God to put aside natural feelings and to submit—even though it is humbling and difficult for him to do so. *God said to Abraham, be not displeased because of the lad and because of your slave-woman; whatever Sarah says to you, do as she tells you, for through Isaac shall your descendants be named* (v. 12).

When Paul, so steeped in patriarchal lore, wrote to both husbands and wives, 'Be subject to one another out of reverence for Christ' (Eph. 5.21), he may have been thinking of the history of Abraham and Sarah with its lessons for succeeding generations. It is a pity that the natural social structures which so rigidly established male dominance were so strong that this remarkably decisive breakthrough into a healthy kind of woman's liberation under the word of God was taken so little notice of even among Abraham's posterity. But in a Church where women are more and more being taken into counsel and seriously listened to, it can encourage us to find such an early signpost clearly pointing in the way we are going.

'As at that time . . . so . . . now'

St Paul found in his day that what happened in the home of Abraham was repeated in what was happening in the churches in Galatia: 'as at that time . . . so it is now' (Gal.

4.29). He wrote to them recalling the irreconcilable conflicts between Sarah and Hagar and between Isaac and Ishmael.

The conflict that took place in Galatia was between the gospel which they had believed in when they first received Christ, and another 'gospel' with which false preachers were trying to oust it. At the beginning the Galatians, following Paul, had put their faith in the promise of God, as Abraham had done. Jesus, they believed, had liberated them from any obligation to do anything more to retain his favour than simply to keep their faith in him, not to grieve or quench the gracious work of the Spirit of God within them. But false preachers had arrived who insisted that Paul had not given them the whole truth. Circumcision according to the law was necessary for salvation. The way to please God was to honour his commandments, always making the utmost effort to keep them all. Human beings had it in their own power to discern the truth and to say yes or no to it. Human initiative, human effort, human works—'the flesh'—had a decisive part to play.

The Galatians were trying to live with both 'gospels'. But Paul saw that the two ways were irreconcilable, and he wrote trying to win them back by urging them to have no traffic or communion with the false teaching. It was from this story in Genesis that he drew one of his chief illustrations. He saw Isaac as the child of the promise and of the free woman Sarah, the gift of grace, of divine initiative, of waiting on God, of receptivity to the work of the Spirit of God. He saw Ishmael as the child of the law and of the bondwoman Hagar, the product of human initiative and human scheming, of the refusal of man to wait on God and take God's way, of the exercise of self-will, of the 'flesh' working contrary to the Spirit of God. Sarah and her child belonged to the new and liberated Jerusalem pictured often in glowing terms in the Prophets. Hagar and her child belonged to Mount Sinai in Arabia, the country into which she was expelled, and to those who crucified Christ and took possession of Jerusalem itself when he died. Salvation for the Galatian Church now depended on appreciating Sarah's insight into this irreconcilable conflict and obeying her injunction: 'Cast out the slave and her son' (Gal. 4.21–31).

At the time of the Reformation, the Reformers felt that this incident spoke to their own situation in the Church as directly as it had to Paul's: 'There are two kinds of persons in the Church' (Calvin). They saw in Ishmael, mocking and persecuting Isaac, a foreshadowing of how the Roman Church of their day, claiming falsely to be the true 'first born' because it looked older, boasting with human pomp of its superior works and wisdom, would persecute the true Church which for comfort could only look away from its own weakness to the word and vindication of God alone. But, they pointed out, truth was not on the side of the strong and boastful. The persecuted could take hope. The sons of the bondwoman cannot eventually dominate that of the free. Isaac's day will come and Ishmael will be cast out. So they urged the persecuted minorities in Europe to endure, for their praying and crying would be heard by God.

What about us today? Possibly we are not in a position to pinpoint so exactly what Ishmael stands for in the world around us. But it is good for us always to ask ourselves whether there is not something of Ishmael, the child of the bondslave, within us. We are prone to slip fatally into behaviour inspired by things and ideas other than the gospel. We live by our own 'principles', our fears, our self-seeking. Periodically we have to search 'the springs of our action' in order to cast out what is bringing us into a bondage other than to God himself.

It is good for us, too, to be aware of how easily the son of the bondwoman can work havoc within the Church. There are times when attitudes and traditions alien to the word of God can win widespread allegiance, harden, create a party loyalty at first critical and gradually becoming more and more antagonistic to certain aspects of the teaching of the word on the freedom of the Spirit, on the grace of God and on the servant form of the people of God. And so we could have the old situation all over again. It is better for us to warn ourselves before it happens, to pray always that it may not happen and to keep a watchful eye—like Sarah and Paul.

14

The Sacrifice of Ishmael

GENESIS 21.14–21

A costly and vexing demand

Abraham found it desperately hard to do God's will and to put out Hagar and Ishmael as Sarah demanded. *The thing was very displeasing to Abraham because of his son* (v. 11). He had already had to face a costly parting from his own kindred when he left Haran. But now, could God really demand this too? He had for so long allowed his heart to grow round the child in natural affection and also in the hope that he might inherit the promise. It was costly to his pride as well as to his love to have to submit to Sarah. It was even more costly because he did not see how it could possibly turn out for the best. Therefore it was only in an act of blind submission to God's command that he gave in.

No doubt, too, he was troubled in conscience. He could see it only as deeply questionable from an ethical point of view for him to have to put out of his home with his child a woman whom he had encouraged to trust him and for whose burdens in life he had a heavy moral responsibility. He had aimed at the highest ideals for the kind of faithfulness and loyalty that should be shown in all human relationships and especially within the family. He had always expected the best from others, and he had been critical when they had fallen short (cf. Gen. 14.23). But now he himself was apparently being forced down to a level he had formerly despised. He had never before imagined that his folly could have brought about a situation in which he would have to fail another person so badly.

This incident is a prelude to the final test he will have to undergo when the demand comes for the sacrifice of Isaac too. Throughout his life we have seen him led from one stage to another in the strength and joy of his faith and self-dedication to God. We now see more clearly that, with increasing cost, he is also being led from one sacrifice to another. At first he had to put on the altar his kith and kin, his country, his settled career. Now it is his pride, his conscience, many of his dearest hopes and some of his tenderest affections that he is being asked for—all this quite late in his life—and there is a more costly test still to come!

Preachers sometimes stress the completeness and the cost of the surrender we have to make of ourselves to God at the beginning of the Christian life—when we 'give ourselves to Jesus' and 'decide' for him. This is a healthy beginning, yet Paul points out that there were stages in our Lord's own life of sacrifice. The first was when he 'emptied himself', took 'the form of a servant' and was 'born in the likeness of men'. The second was when 'in human form' he 'humbled himself' to begin his obedience 'even to death on a cross' (Phil. 2.7–8). The way it happens to us will have some resemblance to the way it happened to him, and Abraham is an earlier example of it.

Confirmation and assurance

I will make a nation of the son of the slave woman also, because he is your offspring (v. 13). This is a repetition of the promise God had already given to Hagar about Ishmael (Gen. 15.10). Moreover it is given with the same emphatic accent, and it comes with the same force, as the promise that had originally taken him out of Haran. 'I will make of you a great nation' (Gen. 12.2), God had then said, and God had not let him down. Now the same God with the same assuring grace is saying, 'I will make of him a nation too!' It is a call to Abraham to put this thing too into God's hands as he had put the other.

Moreover God is saying to him (before he said it to Paul!): 'In everything God works for good with those who love him' (Rom. 8.28). How could any good ever be brought out of something so criminal and stupid as what Abraham had done in the Hagar affair? He had been a fool and he blamed himself. Here he was, beginning to reap a harvest of bitterness from the sin he had sown, and he was afraid of

118

more terrifying consequences as the years passed. Here before him were two people, both dear to himself, who he was condemning to a future hard, empty and frustrating. But now he is told that God will make even this 'good'! Instead of an ugly blot on the final tapestry, there will appear a work of grace and beauty.

Brutal obedience

So much for the promise. If Abraham had not had such a word he could not have faced doing what he had to do, even with all his practised willingness to do God's will. It was actually the grace of God that gave him strength to face what looked on the surface a task unrelievedly harsh.

What Abraham did is told without any attempt to soften its apparent brutality. Some commentators accuse him of callousness. Could he not have softened the blow by at least some acts and words calculated to assure and comfort Hagar? Could he not have made more provision, or provided an escort? And even Luther, Abraham's best fan, at this point is critical: 'Abraham would not have treated the Sodomites more harshly'—though of course he admires Abraham's refusal to argue with God's commands. But others read the text as if it indicated some real love for Hagar and Ishmael, pointing out that the word used for *sent her away* in v. 14 is much softer than the treatment suggested in Sarah's call to 'cast them out' (v. 10). B. Jacob gives a gentle interpretation of what Abraham did: 'Abraham gave Hagar bread and water, probably instructing her to use them sparingly, then he arranges them carefully on her shoulders so that her hands are free. At least we can say that he gave his slave her freedom, and put her on the direct and clear road to her own home country. Finally he places the child in her hands.'

Possibly the harshness in the narrative is deliberate, as the narrator, in speaking so baldly, is simply reminding us in his own way of how obedience to the commands of God can at times force us to seem to be cruel. Perhaps indeed the story is told in such a way as to convey always to its readers the same kind of demand as Jesus pressed on his hearers in his words, 'If any one comes to me and does not hate his own father and mother and wife and children and brothers and sisters, yes, and even his own life, he cannot be my disciple' (Luke 14.26). Abraham was aware too that to try to cover over the stark face of what had to be done by superficial courtesies would merely add to the deep offensiveness of the whole proceedings; it would in no way mitigate the blow that had to be inflicted on his own pride and on the heart of Hagar. For if there are occasions in our own lives when we have to face becoming involved in the kind of action that brings deep and sometimes unexplainable hurt to those who looked for something from us other than what we had to give them, then we must remember it may hurt them the more to find us with a suave and gentle face, when basically we are doing to them something quite brutal. It is as we watch Abraham especially at this point that we can see his trial as a preliminary to the great final testing when he has to sacrifice his son Isaac, too—on the altar.

God takes over

God took over from Abraham not simply in the matter of his conscience but also in the case of Hagar and Ishmael. Hagar soon finds herself at breaking point. One or two commentators suggest that it was by her own fault that she became so lost, that Abraham had given her careful instructions and arranged to meet her again, but that she herself in offended pride took her own way and lost touch. She gives way to wild feelings. 'Despair', said Luther, 'makes her deaf, dumb, blind and thoughtless.' She cannot bear to see the child die at her side, but she cannot bear to abandon him; perhaps clinging to some hope that help may come at the last moment, she lays him in a shady place and goes apart to be within earshot and to weep. But the child has caught something of her own mood and echoes her despair too in expressing his own pain.

And God heard the voice of the lad (v. 17): this verse says something about God. We have already read about how the cry of the oppressed and outraged in Sodom reached his ear

(18.20) and about how he listened to Abraham's intercessions (19.29). Now we see him reached by the sight and sound of a child's tears—and moved with such pity that he sends his angel to save. It says something about the prayer that can move him to answer. It need not always be well phrased or well based theologically. The cry of the human heart, hardly knowing what it is doing but pouring itself out to whoever will hear in its desperate need, is sometimes enough.

He sends the answer through Hagar as well as through an angel. She must take things in hand and become alert. No miracle is needed: she has it all there before her if she will only look around where she has been led. She must no longer allow her despair to blind her. *Arise, lift up the lad, and hold him fast with your hand; for I will make him a great nation* (v. 18). It is the repetition of the promise she has already been given, and also of the promise already given to Abraham. What more can God sometimes say to us than repeat the great things he has already said—if only we will deign to listen? Then God opens her eyes. She hears, holds on, looks and sees.

15
The Well, the Oath and the Tree
GENESIS 21.22–34

A new quandary

At the heart of the promises God made to Abraham from the start there is a twofold theme: his successors have to come from his own seed and they are to be given the land of Canaan. Much of the story of his life as it has been told to us here has been taken up with the question of his successor, and only after much tormenting delay, heart-searching,

prayer and conflict—and by the sacrifice of Ishmael too—
has it been finally settled.

But now Abraham's mind naturally turns to the promise
of the land. As yet he has been given not one concrete sign
that this land is to belong to his successors. He has not been
allowed even to settle permanently on a plot of it. Everything
has seemed to deny this aspect of the promise. How much
longer can God go on repeating the old promises about the
blessing, yet keeping the people to whom they were given in
the condition of landless wanderers? Surely the God who
has given him Isaac will allow him at least a sign that this
land will become their home and possession?

All these questions torment him now no less than the
question of his successor had previously done. And it may
have been this that drove him to dig a well for himself at
Beersheba. Why, at least, could he not have this kind of
possession as a family centre within easy access too for
Ishmael to come back around him sometimes? He no doubt
went to great expense over it. Surely God and his foreign
neighbours would not deny him and his family this one
corner!

But his claim is disputed. The well is claimed for
Abimelech king of Gerar by Phicol the commander of his
army, and Abraham is ordered to desist. He must have been
hurt and despondent, especially in the aftermath of the
Ishmael-Sarah affair. He is either too ashamed or too afraid
to take the matter up directly with Abimelech. He has no
claim whatever upon him and no apparent right to do what
he had done. He was once before rebuked severely by
Abimelech. He does not want the local ruler again to think
he is a trouble-maker. Moreover he can remember how
badly he bungled when he tried to take initiative over the
birth of a son in his family (16.1 ff.). Is this well, in the eyes
of God himself, to be regarded as the disobedient act of an
unbelieving heart?

The word of God—through Abimelech

Yet God steps in just at the moment Abraham needs him most; suddenly everything changes, and what he has done turns out for good. Abimelech himself is moved in heart to come to meet him. Abraham alone of the two feels he knows why he has come, for only a divine hand and a gracious God could have brought this about (Prov. 21.1). His hope is confirmed when he hears Abimelech's first words. God is now beginning to open doors around him so that he and his family can find some settled place in the land. 'God . . . comforted us', said Paul, 'by the coming of Titus' (2 Cor. 7.6).

If an angel had come directly from God he could not have brought more comfort and encouragement. Abraham has recently heard Sarah's voice, as if it were the voice of God. Now he hears Abimelech with the same divine accent. His word *God is with you in all that you do* (v. 22) must have brought to Abraham as much joy as if God himself had appeared and spoken in person.

We ourselves have to be content with finding it this way between us and God, and with leaving it this way. Certainly God can still open the heavens if he wills, and strange things can still happen. But so often it seems to happen entirely through the human medium and on the human level: not directly from heaven but through the Bible—through the preaching, the reading, the discussion—when we have no heavenly vision before our eyes or mind, but simply a friend who has taken the trouble to come and visit us because somehow there was a feeling that drew him, or the pastor in the pulpit who repeats the promises that God once made to his people from his own lips.

And if we can take comfort that this is the way in which God communicates most often with us today, surely we can also utter the hope and the prayer in our heart that sometimes, or perhaps often, he can use us as he did Abimelech.

New avenues of hope

The coming of Abimelech to Abraham of itself opens up new avenues of hope. Now he will raise the matter of the well, and if only he can persuade Abimelech to accept some payment and receive from him some acknowledgement of ownership then he will take this foothold in the land as a sign from God that his children after him will truly possess it. God knows his thoughts, and such a confirmation will be all he can have desired.

It is made easy for him to press his claim. Abimelech has come on a peace errand seeking an alliance with him, for he has been impressed by all the reports he has heard of this stranger and all that he had seen of his ways. *Now therefore swear to me here by God that you will not deal falsely with me or with my offspring or with my posterity, but as I have dealt loyally with you, you will deal with me and with the land where you have sojourned* (v. 23). It seems to Abraham like a fresh prophecy that he and his posterity are not destined to remain in future merely as strangers in the place. So he swears his oath and complains about his treatment in the affair of the well.

Luther at this point makes a very simple comment which applies very cogently to those of us who tend to become victims of neglect or arrogance from sub-officials in a modern bureaucracy. Abimelech had not known what was going on in his kingdom: *I do not know!* (v. 26). 'A godly government', says the Reformer, 'demands that it be informed by its subjects if there is any fault anywhere, for how can it know what is being done everywhere?' It is a plea for appeal tribunals and ombudsmen. We must not too meekly accept the faults of officialdom.

Abraham has the payment for the well out of his pocket. Sheep and oxen are thrust upon the astonished monarch, and a covenant is made acknowledging Abraham's ownership; and to make assurance doubly sure seven ewe lambs are specially set apart as a sign to impress upon Abimelech that it is Abraham who dug the well.

Now Abraham has a sign from God and a pledge from

man that help to sustain his hope in the promise of the land.
He expresses his new-found confidence by planting a tamar-
isk tree and calling *on the name of the Lord, the Everlasting
God* (v. 33). In his joy he has found a new name for his God
to add to *El Shaddai* (Gen. 17.1 ff.), *El Elyon* (Gen. 14.19)
and *El Roi* (Gen. 16.13). This time it is *El Olam*, the
Everlasting God (v. 33) in the sense that he is the God of all
the ages of this earth from the whole past right into the
whole future, however long things will last. 'Thou art the
same, and thy years have no end. The children of thy
servants shall dwell secure; their posterity shall be established before thee' (Ps.102.27–8).

A new approach to conquest

The planting of the tree (v. 33) as a further sign of Abraham's
claim to the land is the climax of a whole series of actions
that reveal on the part of Abraham a determined yet quite
non-combatant approach to the conquest of this land. When
he heard from God that this land was to be his we saw how
he first built his altars (12.7–8), then perambulated its
circumference, wandering over it, pitching his tent here and
there and building other altars. He entered alliances with his
neighbours, made covenants with them, prayed for their
good will and rejoiced, as in this chapter, when he found it.
He builds a well; and now finally he plants a tree.

This is not the way of a man who is imagining that in the
future it will be by sword and fire that he will have to come
into his own. Ultimately it had to come to this. The peoples
of the land persisted in ways of life totally alien to God and
his word. They set their minds and hearts on the total
extermination of the people of God, and there could be no
other answer to them than that of war. But God had in his
mind other ways of conquest that Abraham in his early days
understood well. As with Abimelech and himself there could
be mutual trust and understanding, a sharing of the fear of
the One God, the prayers of the people of God for their
neighbours and the turning of the heart of the neighbour
towards the truth. All this began to happen when Abraham

was in Gerar. Abraham is the kind of man who prefers the altar to the sword, even as a weapon of conquest. War tends especially to destroy the trees (Deut. 20.19); Abraham plants them. War tends especially to poison the wells: Abraham builds them.

16
The Sacrifice of Isaac
GENESIS 22.1–24

How far can human nature go?

After these things God tested Abraham (v. 1). These words are meant to grip our attention in an unusually intense way. Everything that has so far happened to Abraham is now relegated simply to a list of incidents called 'these things'. The climax has now to take place. Everything else has been a building up to what is now to happen. Our concern for Abraham is aroused, as our attention is arrested, for he is now to be brought to a trial which makes us grateful that never again will it ever be quite like this for any of us ordinary men and women, such is its stark horror and crushing loneliness.

It is when we know the New Testament that we can understand more fully than otherwise how God put Abraham to such a test at this stage of his life. A people of God are to come from his seed and acknowledge him as the father of their nation and their faith. The history of this people is to move towards the coming of One, born of the line of Abraham, who is to be willing to go to all lengths, even to the cross, trusting and serving God in obedient love. He has to be willing to say in his Gethsemane: 'Father: if it be possible, let this cup pass from me; nevertheless, not my will, but thine be done' (Matt. 26.39; Luke 22.42).

If Abraham and his successors are going to become a people within whose family life such a One is to be reared, and from whose traditions such a One is to learn, then they too must learn beforehand by the experience of centuries what it means to trust in God and to obey him when the most humiliating and agonizing demands are being made upon them. Their history must even in some faint way contain hints and foreshadowings of the trials and sufferings of the One who is to come, and also some understanding of the meaning of such trials and sufferings. Therefore the way God must take with Abraham and his successors is to be a way of unquestioning obedience through strange and demanding sacrifice and suffering.

Abraham himself at the outset is now to be made a special example of such obedience in willingly accepting and making sacrifice. Already he has proved that he can respond without question. What kind of strain can he now begin to take? How far is he willing to go in unconditional obedience and trust? God, without waiting any more, is going to find and bring it all out in Abraham so that the people who come after him will understand and become strengthened and encouraged.

The God who can wait for the proof

That God 'tests Abraham' seems to mean that he has been waiting for such a proof as he is now to seek, and that he did not know from the start. For it is with a cry of delighted surprise that the climax comes in verse 12: *Now I know that you fear God*. Of course we could read this as a cry of delighted fulfilment, believing that God already knew the potential was fully there and simply created the conditions in which it came to full expression—for how can God really delight in what is not yet expressed?

But the incident is more profoundly and accurately interpreted if we take it that the 'test' was made because God really wanted to find out which way he could take. Even with all his power to work things his way, to overcome human opposition and weakness, God has at times to feel

127

the ground, test over a sustained period of time the people he is going to work with, and he is prepared if need be to alter his plans.

But God is working with human nature, and with human nature there are many things still at stake. There are the questions, by whom and how long? Because God is so free and sovereign, so reliable in his determination to bring about his purpose and so independent of any one human being or any group of human beings, he has the power to wait from generation to generation for the answer to such questions— if he has to. And he has the patience to test his people from generation to generation for the answers—if he has to. It is the crowning glory of Abraham's life that when he was tested God did not have to wait—*Now I know that you fear God!* (v. 12).

We would do well to think sometimes about God and our own potentialities in the light of what is suggested in this verse. It would make the relationship between ourselves and God flat indeed if, in his eyes as they look upon us, there are no imponderables about us and if we felt it really was impossible either to disappoint him or to please him or even utterly to surprise him. Can our 'pleasing' of God not sometimes mean that we offer him a response he could never have calculated from his previous estimates of the hidden springs of our actions?

We would do well to think about God and our own sufferings sometimes in the light of what is suggested in this verse. Of course the idea that God is testing us cannot possibly provide an adequate explanation for the sufferings that come our way. But sometimes it can give us a helpful clue to one line of thought. There is not the least doubt that the trial of Abraham here has been preserved for us in such a vivid story form because it is the kind of trial that each member of the people of God will at some time, though in some lesser degree, have to undergo. When we ourselves, then, are being put through this type of experience, in what kind of hands are we to imagine ourselves? Can the hands that hold us possibly be thought of as inflexible, iron, unyielding, concerned only to mould what is held as if it were mere clay? Or are they to be thought of as tender, sensitive, sympathetic and ready to open up so that some fresh individual or surprising expression can be looked for from what is held within? Can our 'pleasing' of God not sometimes mean that we respond to him with a willingness to offer ourselves as a sacrifice of praise to him in our suffering in such a way that our trust brings him a new honour that he had not sought?

However we think it out, at least we know that he delights no less than we ourselves do in seeing the proof of what he hopes for. It is as if the potential is there and the desire is there—and God knows it is all there—but when it all actually begins to happen, is there not a fresh joy that comes to God? We may sing fervently about the whole realm of nature being an offering far too small in response to his amazing love. And he accepts our praise because we really feel it. But how much greater his joy, how thrilling—and perhaps surprising—to God it can be when we really begin to produce the proof. For then he begins to 'know' in a new way that indeed we fear him.

Call and surrender

The same intense expectation and deep concern as was aroused in us by the writer's introduction was aroused in Abraham by the way he heard his name called on that dreadful morning: Abraham! Sometimes when people come to tell us things that are going to shock us we know it before they even speak or more fully articulate their thoughts. The look on their face or their hesitant fumbling for the right words as they deliberately force themselves into speech can convey the news that has to come. God conveyed something of what was to come and something of his concern for the man who was to hear it in the solemnity and anxiety vibrant in the way he spoke the name.

And at the very beginning—before anything else was done or said—Abraham was able to settle everything. There and then the surrender was total: *Here am I!* (v. 11). It meant, 'I am now as I have always been ready to receive whatever

129

my Lord gives, ready to give whatever my Lord takes.' Now Abraham will be held to God, whatever the coming demand may be. In heart and mind he has already yielded everything. Whatever he is now asked to sacrifice he will have already offered. However great the struggle to yield it again, the outcome is already decided. We would be happy indeed in the sense of being blessed indeed (cf. Matt. 5.1 ff.) if we could follow him in this giving of our very selves to the Lord (2 Cor. 8.5; cf. Luke 1.38).

The meaning of the command

When Abraham finally *took the knife to slay his son* (v. 10), he was going to do it because he believed God had told him very clearly and precisely to do it. There are those who say that this time at least he had tragically misinterpreted the voice and was deluded in thinking that such a demand could ever have come to him from God himself. For them the main point in the story is that God intervened on Mount Moriah at the last moment in order to teach Abraham that child sacrifice was abhorrent to his nature—a thing he had never commanded nor could command. We must admit that especially after our reading of the New Testament our mind naturally shrinks from the idea that God could at any stage of human history, or for any good purpose, have really ordered a father to slay his own son as a sacrifice. But the view that the chief purpose of this incident was the abolition of child sacrifice in Israel robs the incident of its depth of meaning and leaves sections of it incoherent with the whole. If the narrator had meant even to underline such a message it seems doubtful that he would have begun by stating so clearly that God commanded the sacrifice of Isaac, and by inserting such a command in sequence with a whole series of others, each of which he obviously means us to take as having been given without a trace of hesitation or ambiguity.

Take your son, your only son Isaac, whom you love, and go to the land of Moriah, and offer him there as a burnt offering (v. 2). Neither Abraham nor anyone else in that world would have thought of raising even in his own mind the question whether God had a right to demand such a sacrifice or whether man could possibly be in the wrong to give it. Abraham himself was a morally upright man and quick to protest even to God against anything he felt was scandalous and unjust (cf. 14.23; 18.25). It was a world where even good people sacrificed human beings and thought that under certain circumstances they were right to do so. From early times, especially in great emergencies, people had believed that when things went wrong the situation could be helped to come right again if a sacrifice in the form of animal or plant life was offered; in special emergencies, where the most effective kind of sacrifice was required, they believed that they had to offer the most precious thing in life—the fruit of the human womb. It was not till after the time of Abraham that child sacrifice was specifically forbidden in the law of Israel (Deut. 18.10), and so strongly rooted in the human mind was the belief in it that it was practised in Israel up till the time of the exile to Babylon and was regarded even by those who did not practise it themselves as something that was bound to have an uncanny and very powerful effect on the control of human affairs (cf. 2 Kings 3.27).

Let us try then to imagine Abraham's thoughts after he heard himself commanded to do such a thing to Isaac. Is it not likely that he felt that such a sacrifice was necessary on his part in order to help to put right what had gone so deeply and tragically wrong with human life? For now at this stage of his life, he was beginning to realize how far things had gone wrong and how long it was going to be before things changed in human life as a whole.

What price had now to be paid for the complete fulfilment of the promise? He had seen the havoc that could be worked by his own folly in his home. He had seen the havoc worked by evil in Sodom. How could such evil be arrested and things be put right again? Might not this sacrifice have something to do with such a cure? Might it not be his own supreme role to pay it? As for his son Isaac, might it not be his great part to submit? And if he did so would God not

131

honour him and raise him up as he accepted the sacrifice (cf. Heb. 11.19)?

Such may have been Abraham's thoughts. But we are told little in the story about what anyone thought that day. Therefore all we can do in interpreting it is to struggle as best we can, with honesty, prayer and consistency, to use our imagination—as well as our biblical knowledge—as we try to enter sympathetically into the situation. But if the custom of sacrificing children was abhorrent to God and could not save the human situation, was it justifiable for God to lead Abraham into such a train of thought and to give him the agony of having to decide to do it when it was all to be revoked?

Some commentators on this point emphasize strongly that what God wanted to have was not the sacrifice of Isaac, but the personal total surrender of Abraham. Marcus Dods says that God meant Abraham to make the sacrifice in spirit and not in the outward act. He could not know he had Abraham's own total surrender of himself till he had brought him to the point of slaying Isaac. (We will discuss a deeper justification for what God did in leading him on to this extent.)

Facing the cost

The writer emphasizes the intensity of the pain Abraham had to bear both at the moment of the command and throughout the long journey. We cannot adequately compare his trial to that of our own when we in our tragic experience of bereavement have to yield our dear ones up to God as he himself seems to take them from us. Abraham is here being asked not simply to say as Job did: 'The Lord gave, and the Lord has taken away, blessed be the name of the Lord' (Job 1.21). He is being commanded to engage in the very act of immolating his own son; he himself must preside over and perform the sacrifice. He had seen often enough the strange horror of approaching death in the eyes and struggling of the animals he had killed for such sacrifice. Possibly in his early life he had seen it in the human victims too in Ur and Haran.

The command to obey seemed itself aimed to touch him as deeply as possible at the heart of his tender human affection: *Take your son, your only son Isaac whom you love . . . and offer him* (v. 2). The demand for *your only son* seems to be calculated to remind him of what it felt like to sacrifice Ishmael, his other dear child. Is God going to leave him now with nothing? But this man is to be torn not only at the point of his deepest natural feelings. The command seems to threaten everything he has lived for, fought and prayed for, from the moment he left Haran. Then he had sacrified his past for the hope of the glorious promised future. Now he seems to be asked to sacrifice the future too, for all his hopes are now embodied in his child. In sacrificing Isaac it seems as if he has to sacrifice even the promise.

The long journey

The length of the journey prolongs the agony beforehand. Even on the third day Abraham lifts up his eyes to see the place still 'afar off' (v. 4). The journey towards an agony can become as painful as the agony itself. We are not meant to try to understand even the passion and crucifixion of Jesus as the sudden infliction of a pain, horror or dereliction not felt or borne in some incomprehensible way beforehand. Perhaps it began for Jesus even in childhood; but it was certainly there, beginning to thrust itself upon him from the day he allowed himself to be baptized into it by John the Baptist (Mark 1.9), and he was already 'dwelling in his passion' when he 'set his face to go to Jerusalem' (Luke 9.51).

The isolation of Abraham in his own thoughts is emphasized. He has to separate himself from the servants, who could not have begun to understand what was taking place. Symbolically he lays the wood on the child. He himself carries only the knife and the fire in his own hand. But he himself knows the heavy inner burden. The child hardly knows, hardly thinks. It will be enough to have to watch the agony in the child when the moment arrives. Yet there is a strangely binding and drawing fellowship between himself and the child indicated in the phrase: *So they went both of them together* (v. 6). How stern and grim it all is. These were stern and grim days—but Christ has brought a difference.

Question and answer

Though the deep fellowship between the father and the son was there in the long silences, the one question and the one answer reveal what both were now feeling. When Abraham is addressed as 'my father' in simple childlike trust, almost involuntarily there comes to expression before the child what Abraham is trying to say again to his own heavenly Father as he walks along that road: *Here am I, my son* (v. 7). He has had to say it again and again and again, and God knows it is being said to him as well as to the child. For continually to present our own selves as a living sacrifice to God (Rom. 12.1) is the best way to become able to face whatever other sacrifices must go along with it.

And now it comes out that Isaac too has begun to share something of Abraham's own questioning and agony. Can it be simply innocent chatter, or is he beginning to express the tormenting thought of his own father? *Behold, the fire and the wood; but where is the lamb for a burnt offering?* (v. 7). Is the mind of Isaac not beginning even now to orient itself to the thought that he himself may be the victim?

The answer is sincere. Abraham is not trying to cover over his doubts. It is a noble confession of his faith in the goodness of God. B. Jacob thinks that Abraham had forestalled the question and had prepared the answer beforehand in his mind: *'God will provide himself the lamb for a burnt offering, my son* (v. 8). Is it not better to think of the answer as being inspired by the question—the father as being helped by his son? For there is no doubt that Abraham's faith rises to wonderful heights within this fellowship of question and answer. Whatever the answer meant, for it can have many meanings, it expresses 'his complete certainty of God, together with complete openness as to detail' (Kidner). If Abraham had only known it (but how can *we* ever forget it?), the heavenly Father was already running to meet him with deep and tender compassion so that he could fall on his neck to kiss him (Luke 15.20).

'On the mount of the Lord'

The act that follows can be interpreted only as having been done with the deliberate intention of going through with it. There was not a hint of sham or play-acting in Abraham as he *built an altar there and laid the wood in order, and bound Isaac his son, and laid him on the altar, upon the wood* (v. 9). 'I could not have been an onlooker, much less the performer or the player', says Luther; and this is where most of us stand.

Suddenly divine intervention comes—at the moment he *put forth his hand and took the knife to slay his son* (v. 10). So determined is he to obey, so grimly intent on what he has to do that his name has to be called quickly and twice before he lifts up his eyes and sees the ram caught in the thicket by his horns (v. 13). And now he understands the meaning of what he was inspired to say to Isaac in answer to his question— 'The Lord will provide'—and he gives the place this name (v. 14). And now he sees more deeply than ever he has seen before into the heart and life of God, and into the meaning of our human life itself.

Later generations, when they told and discussed this story, summed up its message in the phrase that could mean either 'On the mount of the Lord it shall be provided' or 'On the mount of the Lord, he shall be seen' (v. 14 text and margin). Obviously it was as they allowed the story to unfold itself from this point that they felt they were able to see its fullest depth of meaning and its most striking relevance to life.

Von Rad insists that this incident has very many levels of meaning and makes lofty demands on the thought of its readers; and he suggests that 'when Israel read this story in later times, it could only see itself represented by Isaac, i.e. laid on Yahweh's altar, given back to him, then given life again by him from above'. That is to say, Israel could base its existence in history not on its own legal titles as other nations did, but only on the will of him whom in the freedom of his grace permitted Isaac to live.

B. Jacob, the Jewish commentator, prefers to translate the phrase we are discussing as 'On the mount of the Lord it shall be seen', and he writes,

> There everything is revealed. 'God sees' is the essence of religion, creating fear of him and confidence in him. To see God is the deepest longing of a soul that is kindred to God. Abraham's story teaches that God is to be experienced in sacrifice, with a certainty that grows as the sacrifice becomes greater. Moriah is a summit of religious experience. It will be seen. The subject is intentionally not mentioned. Everything stands revealed there; both the character of the man who goes there, as well as the essence of the divine.

If this story of the sacrifice of Isaac helped Israel as a nation in later difficult times to understand something of its own history, and to have confidence in God when he seemed to be contradicting himself and almost destroying his own work, it can help us still today. It can help us to endure the demands God has already made on us with the certainty that at the crucial time, when no more can be asked for, he will accept us and we will be able to see it all. It can help us to face the sacrifice of what he is asking us to give. Many people have found this incident helped them more than any other in the Bible when somehow a call from God seemed to cut deeply across the ties that bound them to someone who was naturally dear to them, or seemed to demand the very costly sacrifice of something that in itself was one of the good things in their lives—perhaps the best thing, as Isaac was to Abraham. But by the grace of God they were able to face it, and it was in the very act of obedience that what was offered was given back to them, and the whole relationship that had been threatened took on a new depth of meaning.

The mystery

We cannot leave this story without a discussion of what it has said to generations of Christians about Christ, and especially about his passion and his relation to God. When John the Baptist pointed to Jesus and said, 'Behold the lamb of God', he may have been thinking of the story of the Passover lamb or of the verse in Isaiah 53.7: 'He was led like a sheep to the slaughter.' But also he may have had in mind this story.

Some commentators have looked at Isaac's role in particular, and those who find important significance in the striking similarities they can catch between events in the New Testament and those in the Old draw attention to the correspondence between Isaac carrying the wood of the sacrifice, as a sentenced man carries his own cross, and Jesus, who after he was sentenced 'went out, bearing his own cross, to the place called the place of a skull' (John 19.17). This, of course, could be purely outward coincidence. But when we probe behind the outward similarity, at the same time remembering the deep unity of spirit and life between the New Testament and the Old, the typology no longer seems to be merely trivial. In this whole incident Isaac's obedient and passive self-offering is as remarkable as that of Abraham. And in this he proves himself the child of the promise. He seems to yield himself in complete trust into the hands of his father and of his God. He allows himself to be bound and lays himself on the altar. As he yields himself he seems to be in a deep at-one-ness with his father, who, he seems to sense, is at the same time making an offering as costly as his own. Kidner asks us to note in this connection the significance of the phrase 'So they went, both of them together' (v. 8).

Isaac's attitude leads us on in thought to the description of the suffering servant of Isaiah 53.7: 'Like a lamb that is led to the slaughter, and like a sheep that before its shearers is dumb, so he opened not his mouth.' And at this point of course we are caught up deeply and firmly in the movement of the Old Testament towards him 'who through the eternal

Spirit offered himself without blemish to God' (Heb. 9.14). The later life of Isaac must be judged against this background. We may find him always passive, unadventurous and lacking in initiative. Deep faults come out, for he is very human, but in the end he comes back, and he deserves to be the heir of his father Abraham.

Some of these Old Testament stories, like this one before us, have vast, cathedral-like inner structures. When you have spent hours looking at even one aspect with a mind fascinated by its rich detail and symbolism and craftsmanship, you can leave it to look at some other aspect of the building. But then when you go back to where you were before, you suddenly find some new avenue to discovering what its builders were intending to say, just where you thought you had already seen everything there was to see. So here, now, having visited the Isaac chapel we come back for a moment to the Abraham chapel, to look again at this man who was also offering himself in his offering. All along no doubt there had been in his mind the question: What will it cost the people of God in the service of God to become those through whom all the world is to be blessed? At Mount Moriah he thought that somehow he was beginning to find out. He had already given everything. Was God not now asking for more—so that the price could be more fully paid? And so he offered his lamb, his Isaac; and suddenly God intervened with the substitute. Having brought Abraham to the point of yielding the greatest and best, he said in effect: 'Not your best, Abraham, but mine! Not your lamb, Abraham, but mine! Not your son, but mine!'

17
Walking Towards the End
GENESIS 23.1–20

The acceptance of the end

In the last two or three stories recorded about him we see Abraham, now an old man, immersed in common, ordinary domestic affairs and using shrewd common sense to help solve his problems as he also seeks divine guidance. No visions are given to him. No longer does any voice come from above in dramatic intervention, no deep religious experiences are recorded. He is very much on our own mundane level in what he has to do—to make the funeral arrangements for Sarah when she dies, to find a good wife for Isaac (Gen. 24) and to make a fair disposal of the family property. We discover now that at some stage in his life he had taken a second wife and that there were 'sons of his concubines' (Gen. 25. 1–5). We have to accept this simply as something everybody did without question. It seems to have been so small a part of his later life that nothing ever clouds over the fact that Sarah is his only true wife.

Yet God is as near to this man now, guarding his affairs with as careful an oversight as at any earlier time—a reminder to us that when we become physically less able to cope and are forced more and more into a quiet routine of retirement, there need be no loss of a basic spiritual strength nor of our firm grasp of the unseen. 'The path of the righteous is like the light of dawn, which shines brighter and brighter until full day' (Prov. 4.18). The best wine in the kingdom of God is often served towards the end (John 2). 'They who wait for the Lord', said the prophet, 'shall renew their strength, they shall mount up with wings like eagles, they shall run and not be weary, they shall walk and not faint' (Isa. 40.31). Abraham can no longer soar, or even run! All that is left for him to do is to walk. But God marvellously as ever is with him so that he does not faint.

He is a good example to us for the time when it happens to ourselves. He does not try to bottle up his feelings when Sarah dies. It is healthy to weep and to express our grief. Abraham does it alone before God: *Abraham went in to mourn for Sarah and to weep for her* (v. 2). But had he had another close to him, he would not have been ashamed to show his tears. He does not try to evade facing death and the dead, and he loses no necessary time in doing decently and carefully everything that has to be gone through in arranging for the actual burial and the service.

Of course there were common burial-places around, and the poor vagrants who roamed the countryside had to use them when any of their company died. But Abraham wanted more. He must now purchase a piece of land. His wife's body must be laid in a worthy tomb. His family must have a shrine of some sort here in Canaan. He will go to those who own the land and plead with them for it.

The hope of new beginnings with God

Abraham is not seeking simply to follow the ordinary social customs of people like himself, who had to maintain even in the last rites the dignity and decency of reasonable wealth. He has other reasons for what he wants to do.

We can think back to what he did immediately he arrived in Canaan (cf. p. 13). In full view of the pagan shrine at Shechem he built an altar to the Lord, and in doing so he claimed the whole land for his God and his posterity. Besides building this altar he had already dug a well and planted a tree. The burial-place he will now buy for Sarah will be no less symbolic: it will be another pledge of the future possession of the land for all his successors and an even more decisive beginning of the fulfilment of the promise: *To your descendants I will give this land* (Gen. 12.7). He believes it will help to bind the heart of his successors to the country and thus to the promise.

He has more even than this in his mind. Can we possibly come to know the face of God, as Abraham came to know him, and not begin to believe that not even death can separate us from that love? Is God going to allow himself to be robbed of his friends by death? Jesus denied such a possibility and pointed out that long after Abraham died, God called himself still the God of Abraham, Isaac and Jacob, implying that Abraham lived with him for ever (Matt. 22.31 f.). B. Jacob suggests that the purchase of the burial-place was made in Sarah's honour by Abraham 'as a testimony of his love beyond death', for he loved her long after she was gone. But it was more. He buried Sarah in this way as a testimony of *God's* love for her beyond death. He is reaching towards the truth that he and his wife and successors are destined in body as well as in spirit for another and a greater life. He is not only claiming that the land belongs to his successors but that resurrection belongs to the body of his wife.

Scholars point out that long after the time of Abraham many Old Testament writers speak in a very gloomy way about how things are to be for us after death. They claim that it was only late in the history of the people of God that the great affirmation we have about resurrection and eternal blessedness was made. If they are right, then Abraham is a pioneer whose faith his successors found too hard to match.

A final venture of faith

Will the people of the land be willing to sell him a burial plot? May he not be snubbed and insulted as he goes, seemingly cap in hand, to ask the favour? May he not encounter even an incipient racial prejudice and be told as an immigrant that he cannot expect too soon all the privileges of long residence? Will they not be acting within reason if they tell him to embalm the body and go back to Haran?

It requires of this physically weak old man, now very sensitive emotionally, a great deal of effort to risk such a result. But he is driven on and made bold by his faith. Possibly it taxes his courage as much as had some of his earlier and more dramatic ventures. We admire his effort as he goes to *ask*, all the more because behind it there is a trembling man, ready to break down and weep and praying to God to help him not to falter. He tries to hold his head high because the servant of such a great God must never jeopardize his honour.

This incident, indeed, appeals to us the more because it applies so directly to what we often have to do—especially if we are church workers. How often in raising funds, for example, do we have to go and *ask*, in the name of Christ, a response from people whose reactions can easily hurt us. How often in our ventures in personal evangelism do we have to sum up courage within a trembling heart in order to be able to speak our faith to other people!

Abraham is tactful in his approach to the Hittites who own the land. He knows that he must not give even the least suspicion that he is doing any more than asking a gracious favour, and his prayer to them begins with an admission that no one owes him anything and that if he is listened and responded to, it will be only because of the graciousness of his kindly hosts. *I am a stranger and a sojourner among you!* It is a frank legal acknowledgement that he has no 'rights' nor the privilege of making such a request. It is an act of personal self-humiliation.

Yet the personal dignity that accompanies the humble petition prevents those he is dealing with from treating him in any cavalier or condescending manner. He is formal, but it is a spontaneous and engaging formality. It has been pointed out that the Hittites address Abraham as 'my Lord' in every speech, but he himself never reciprocates or calls himself their servant. He knows that he is going to have to pay dearly for what he finally purchases, but he speaks of the whole transaction from the start as if it were to be a gracious gift from them to him. Moreover he underlines the fact that he is simply seeking help from them in one of the tragic situations of human need that inevitably visit each and all of us of whatever class or creed or tribe. *I am a stranger and a settler among you. Let me own a burial plot among you so that I may take my dead wife and bury her* (Jerusalem Bible).

How wise and tactful he is! He knows the customs of the

land, and when the business discussion begins he rises from where he has been sitting and bows to the Hittites so that they can start negotiating. He has already shrewdly calculated the kind of price they will want, and he has brought all the money he needs. He knows they will at first insist on his accepting the plot as a gift, and he knows he must show no sign of flinching when they inevitably take advantage of his insistence on paying and his deference about the amount. Their demand is extortionate but he maintains his dignity, indeed his magnanimity, and pays up promptly.

He wins them over! Is he not quietly and impressively evangelizing these people even as he negotiates with them? Such wisdom and tact, such sympathetic understanding of their customs and ways of life, such uncompromising dignity combined with dignified compromise can go far. We can note that the deep personal humility that reflected itself in Abraham's engaging deference before other people was something he received and learned before God in his prayer-life (cf. Gen. 18.27 and 23.4), and in the same place he also discovered that a call to the service of God can enable us to lift up our heads as well as our hearts.

A final word of encouragement

It is obvious that Abraham wins over the Hittites because the way he has already lived his daily life and conducted his daily business affairs with them has made an extraordinary impression. They have watched him for years, and they have recognized something distinct and enviable about this stranger in their midst and his way of life. Their admiration is spontaneously expressed (we take the translation given in the Jerusalem Bible and others to be accurate): *Hear us, my Lord. You are God's prince among us.*

Of course Abraham *is* a 'stranger' to them. He has been distant and reserved, but they respect him for this because they recognize that he belongs to another kind of world than that to which they belong. 'They comprehend that they have before them', writes B. Jacob, 'an extraordinary man belonging to a world in which he is not only a citizen but a

prince; it is an honour to them to have him in their midst.'
Not only do they confess their long-felt admiration for him,
but they give a hint that in spite of the distance between
them and him they like to think of him as belonging to
them—a prince of God *among us!* The very strangeness of
the man and of the spiritual kingdom he belongs to (cf. John
18.36) makes them want to have him as theirs.

How much it means to Abraham undergoing this trial,
and at this stage in his life, to hear all this said to him and to
be given this generous emotional response—far beyond what
he had imagined! Is not God answering his boldest prayers?
And now instead of giving him a vision from heaven or a
supernatural voice, God has put his personal word again into
the mouth of his pagan neighbours—'You are my Prince,
Abraham!' It is the second time such a strong and assuring
word has come to Abraham in his need spoken by the people
around him, but spoken by God. 'Sarah' means 'Princess'.
God had given his dear wife this very special name when the
announcement was made of Isaac's birth (17.15). Now he
knows God is again reminding him of that great though
distant day in the past and assuring him that he never goes
back on any of his promises. It seems to be the final word of
encouragement from God to a servant who had done well
and lived well and is now beginning to find that what a man
sows in faith and goodness he shall also reap.

Acknowledgements

Unless otherwise indicated, the Scripture quotations in this publication are from the Revised Standard Version of the Bible, copyrighted 1946 and 1952 by the Division of Christian Education of the National Council of the Churches of Christ in the USA.

The quotations from Calvin's *Commentary on Genesis* are from the Calvin Society edition, Edinburgh, 1847.

The quotations from Luther are from his *Lectures on Genesis* (Luther's Works, Vols. 2–4), Concordia Publishing House, St Louis, 1960–4.

Recent works consulted and referred to are:

Cassuto, U., *A Commentary on the Book of Genesis*. The Hebrew University, Jerusalem, 1961.

Jacob, B., *The First Book of the Bible, Genesis*. KTAV Publishers, New York, 1974.

Kidner, D., *Genesis* (Tyndale Commentaries). Inter-Varsity Press, London, 1967.

Sarna, N. B., *Understanding Genesis*. Jewish Theological Seminary of America, New York, 1966.

von Rad, G., *Genesis* (Old Testament Library). SCM Press, London, 1972.